G. Margoliouth

Descriptive List of Syriac and Karshuni Mss. in the British Museum Acquired since 1873

G. Margoliouth

Descriptive List of Syriac and Karshuni Mss. in the British Museum Acquired since 1873

ISBN/EAN: 9783744735995

Printed in Europe, USA, Canada, Australia, Japan

Cover: Foto ©Andreas Hilbeck / pixelio.de

More available books at **www.hansebooks.com**

DESCRIPTIVE LIST

OF

SYRIAC AND KARSHUNI MSS.

IN THE

BRITISH MUSEUM

ACQUIRED

SINCE 1873.

BY

G. MARGOLIOUTH, M.A.
ASSISTANT IN THE DEPARTMENT OF ORIENTAL PRINTED BOOKS AND MSS.;
FORMERLY TYRWHITT HEBREW SCHOLAR.

PRINTED BY ORDER OF THE TRUSTEES.

London:
SOLD AT THE BRITISH MUSEUM,
AND BY
MESSRS. LONGMANS & CO., 39, PATERNOSTER ROW; BERNARD QUARITCH,
15, PICCADILLY, W.; ASHER & CO., 13, BEDFORD STREET, COVENT GARDEN;
KEGAN PAUL, TRENCH, TRÜBNER & CO., PATERNOSTER
HOUSE, CHARING CROSS ROAD; AND MR. HENRY FROWDE,
OXFORD UNIVERSITY PRESS WAREHOUSE, AMEN CORNER.

1899

NOTICE.

The MSS. described in the present List were, for the most part, purchased for the Museum by Dr. Budge, Keeper of the Egyptian and Assyrian Antiquities, in 1889 and 1890, at Mōṣul, Alḳōsh, and the Ṭiārī district. Prior to these dates about fifty volumes had been acquired, and several other volumes have been subsequently brought from Urmī and the neighbourhood. It will be seen that, besides a strong element of the classical literature of the Syrians, this collection contains a large number of works written in Karshūni, and that it also includes several volumes of Chaldaean (Roman Catholic) theology. Special attention may be drawn to the examples of modern Syriac literature contained in the collection (see more particularly Or. 4422 and 4423).

The student may note that the S.P.C.K. collection of Syriac and Karshūni MSS. at Cambridge, and also the Sachau collection at Berlin, are in many respects similar in character to the present MSS. This collection has also more features in common with the Oxford and Paris Syriac and Karshūni MSS. (see the

Catalogues of the late Dean Payne Smith and M. Zotenberg) than with the Syriac MSS. of the British Museum described in the Catalogue of the late Professor Wright.

Thanks are due to Mr. W. E. Crum, as well as to several members of the Museum staff, for much valuable help in the identification of the less-known names and titles occurring in the List.

ROBERT K. DOUGLAS,

Keeper of the Department of Oriental Printed Books and MSS.

April, 1899.

DESCRIPTIVE LIST

OF

SYRIAC AND KARSHUNI MSS.

Or. 1240. A number of fragments:—1. St. John i. 31—45 in Ethiopic, Syriac, Coptic, Arabic (in the Syriac character), and Armenian. Paper. xiiith—xivth Century. The single extant leaf is very much mutilated, and of the Ethiopic part only a few letters remain.—2. Several mutilated vellum leaves of the xiith—xiiith Century, containing fragments of homilies.—3. Part of a vellum leaf, in two columns, containing portions of hymns. Jacobite writing of the xth—xith Century.—4. An Armenian fragment on vellum, containing a portion of a homily. xiiith—xivth Century.

Or. 1272. A collection of fragments:—1. Fol. 1, a leaf of the Gospel of St. John, containing ch. xvi. 7 (first word, ܠܘܬܟܘܢ)—20 (last word, ܐܢܬܘܢ), in a large beautiful Esṭrangĕlā of the vith Century. It really belongs to the Brit. Mus. MS. Add. 14,455[a], its position in that MS. being between the last two leaves.—

[a] The leaves noted will now be embodied in Add. 14,455 and 14,552 respectively.

2. Foll. 2—5, containing portions of the Homilies of Cyril of Alexandria on the Gospel of St. Luke, in a flowing hand of the viith or viiith Century. The contents of these leaves, which properly form part of Add. 14,552", were published by the late Prof. William Wright in 1874.—3. Fol. 6, a leaf (of apparently the viith Century) belonging to a collection of Homilies, the heading on the verso being ܬܘܒ. ܦܘܫܩܐ ܕܡܐܡܪ̈ܐ. ܡܢ ܡܬܪܓܡܢܘܬܐ ܕܣܘܝܪܘܣ ܚܣܝܐ; see Or. 2732.—4. Foll. 7 and 8, part of a MS. containing prayers in commemoration of saints; ixth or xth Century.—5. Fol. 9, a viith or viiith Century fragment of the Gospel of St. Matthew in the Peshiṭta version (parts of chs. xix. and xx.).—6. Foll. 10—12, three different mutilated fragments, the first (apparently part of a homily) being written in a beautiful Edessene Esṭrangĕlā of probably the vith Century.*

Or. 1300. The fourth volume of the Homilies of the Priest Emmanuel bar Shahhārē on the Hexaemeron, or six days of Creation, composed partly in heptasyllabic and partly in dodecasyllabic metre. The original number of homilies belonging to this part was twenty-eight, but the second is wanting. See Wright's Syriac Catalogue, pp. 231, 232; also Or. 4072. Paper, foll. 198. Folio. Dated A.GR. 1996 (A.D. 1685).

Or. 1592. The Book of Psalms in the Peshiṭta version; imperfect at the beginning and the end. Paper, foll. 78. Small 4°. xvith Century.

Or. 1593. A treatise on Chemistry and Natural Philosophy, composed partly in Syriac and partly in

* See note on p. 1.

Arabic (Karshuni). Paper, foll. 49. Sm. 4°. xvth Century.

Or. 1594. A Dictionary of the Syriac language, perhaps a recension of that of Ebdochus (*Εὔδοξος*); imperfect at the beginning and end. Paper, foll. 73. Sm. 4°. xvth Century.

Or. 2084. The Prognostics of Daniel (ܟܬܒܐ ܕܫܘܕܥܐ ܕܪܘܒܢܐ ܕܕܢܝܐܝܠ ܢܒܝܐ); two tracts on the prognostics from convulsions (ܙ̈ܘܥܐ), the title of the second being: ܬܢܐ ܐܚܪܢܐ ܕܙ̈ܘܥܐ ܕܕܒܝܬ ܠܚܠܝܡܘܣ ܙܒܢ ܐܣܛܘ̈ܬܐ; the riddles of John Azraḳ, Bishop of Ḥîrtā; a Syriac recension of Aesop's Fables (62 in number; compare S. Hochfeld's "Beiträge zur Syrischen Fabelliteratur," where only 60 are given); and several smaller pieces. Paper, foll. 68. 8°. Dated A.GR. 2067 (A.D. 1756).—Appended are fragments (foll. 69—80) of a work on the interpretation of various dreams, in modern Syriac, belonging to the xixth Century.

Or. 2287. Fragments of the Gospels of St. Mark, St. Luke, and St. John, of the Acts of the Apostles, the Epistle of St. James, and the Pauline Epistles. Peshiṭta version. Vellum, foll. 79. Folio. viiith or ixth Century.

Or. 2288-9. A large portion of the New Testament according to the Peshiṭta version. Vellum, foll. 91 and 107. Folio. ixth or xth Century. The last three leaves of Or. 2289 contain fragments of Judges (xiii. 8 sqq.), 1 Samuel (vi. 15 sqq.), and Ruth (i. 16 sqq.).

Or. 2290. The Psalms according to the Peshiṭta version. Paper, foll. 186. 8°. Dated A.GR. 2158 (A.D. 1847).

Or. 2291. The four Gospels according to the Ḥarklensian version, accompanied by an Arabic translation; imperfect. Paper, foll. 150. Regular but rather inelegant writing of the xiith—xiiith Century.

Or. 2292. A Nestorian Lectionary from the Pauline Epistles; imperfect. Paper, foll. 92. Bold writing of the xivth—xvth Century.

Or. 2293. A collection of Anaphoras (including those of the Apostles; John, Bishop of Ḥarran; Xystus, Bishop of Rome; Basil, Bishop of Bagdad (also known by the names of Philoxenus and Lazarus bar Sābhĕthā); and Jacob of Serūg. The Anaphoras are preceded by introductory portions (*προοίμια*) and followed by concluding hymns (ܚܘܬܡ̈ܐ), which are partly in Syriac and partly in Arabic (Karshuni). Leaves are wanting at the beginning and the end, and also after fol. 98. Paper, foll. 144. Dated (on fol. 116*a*) A.GR. 2041 (A.D. 1730).

Or. 2294. Another collection of Anaphoras (including those of John bar Ma'danī, also known as Aaron bar Ma'danī; Xystus, Bishop of Rome; and Abraham ܢܚܫܝܪܬܢܐ), accompanied by the usual introductory and concluding portions; and also containing short services in connection with new vessels for the altar, &c. Partly Karshuni. Paper, foll. 139. Two different hands; dated A.GR. 2016 (A.D. 1705).

Or. 2295. Another collection of Anaphoras (including those of James, the Brother of the Lord; the twelve

Apostles; Julius of Rome; Matthew the Shepherd; Peter of Callinicus; Gregory Nazianzen). Imperfect. Paper, foll. 159. Dated (on fol. 129*a*) A.GR. 1793 (A.D. 1482).

Or. 2296. A Nestorian Service-book, containing the "Abū Ḥalīm" (so called on account of its having been compiled by Elias III. (Abū Ḥalīm ibn al-Ḥadīthī), catholicos of the Nestorians; see Wright's "Syriac Literature," p. 256), besides various other services (ܠܒܘܫܐ ܕܟܗ̈ܢܐ, ܠܒܘܫܐ ܕܥܡܕܐ ܘܫܪܪ). The MS. is imperfect, and in parts now only legible with difficulty. Paper, foll. 82. Apparently dated A.GR. 1845 (A.D. 1534), but the writing is partly rubbed away.

Or. 2297. The first part of a Choral Service-book. The title appearing in the heading of fol. 1*a* is: ܟܬܒܐ ܕܚܘܕܪܐ ܕܐܝܬܘܗܝ ܟܬܒܐ ܩܕܡܝܐ ܡܢ ܪܫܗ ܕܬܫܪܝܢ ܐܚܪܝܢ ܒܥܒܕܐ ܠܟܠܗ ܕܫܢܬܐ. Paper, foll. 320. Folio. The volume is made up of fragments in different hands belonging to the xvth and xvith Centuries. A number of leaves are more or less mutilated.

Or. 2298. A fragmentary Service-book (ܒܝܬ ܓܙܐ) for the festivals. Paper, foll. 282. Folio. Written in two different hands of apparently the xvth Century, and supplemented by a hand of the xviith Century.

Or. 2299. ܒܥܘܬܐ ܕܢܝ̈ܢܘܝܐ, a Nestorian Service-book used at the commemoration of the three days' fast of the Ninivites. Imperfect. Paper, foll. 134. 8°. Dated A.GR. 1560, A.H. 646 (A.D. 1249).

Or. 2300. Another imperfect copy of the ܒܥܘܬܐ ܕܢܝ̈ܢܘܝܐ. xiiith Century. Foll. 133—161 (bearing the title *ܡܐܡܪܐ ܕܒܬܘܠܬܐ) are in a different hand, dated A.GR. 1793 (A.D. 1482). Paper, foll. 161. 8°.

Or. 2301. A Choral Service-book (part of the ܒܝܬ ܓܙܐ), containing various kinds of hymns for festivals. Imperfect. Paper, foll. 117. Large 8°. xvth—xvith Century.

Or. 2302. ܟܬܒܐ ܕܦܪܕܝܣܐ ܕܥܕܢ, "The Book of the Paradise of Eden," a collection of fifty poems on various theological subjects, by 'Ebed-Yēshū', Metropolitan of Nisibis and of Armenia. Paper, foll. 130. 8°. Dated A.GR. 2005 (A.D. 1694).

Or. 2303. The same work as the preceding. Paper, foll. 88. Folio. Written in a Nestorian hand of the xixth Century.

Or. 2304. A collection of Hymns by Gabriel Ḳamṣā, Metropolitan of Mosul; Khamīs bar Ḳardāḥē, whose hymns are known under the title of ܒܡܫܗ (see e.g. Badger, "The Nestorians," ii. 24); and others. Paper, foll. 178. Large 8°. Dated A.GR. 2188 (A.D. 1877).

Or. 2305. Metrical Discourses illustrative of the tenets of the Nestorians; partly in heptasyllabic and partly in dodecasyllabic metre. Probably composed by John bar Zō'bī (see Wright's "Syriac Literature," p. 258). Imperfect. Paper, foll. 149. Large 8°. xviiith Century.

Or. 2306. The works ascribed to Dionysius the Areopagite, accompanied by the introduction and explanatory notes of Phocas bar Sergius of Edessa, and other writers. Paper, foll. 178. Folio. Copied A.GR. 1859 = A.D. 1548 (fol. 178*a*) from an ancient codex on vellum which was dated (fol. 17*a*) A.GR. 1078 (A.D. 767).

* Compare Cambridge Add. MS. 1981 (S.P.C.K. collection), fol. 40*b*.

Or. 2307. A collection of theological tracts (partly in Karshuni), including Confessions of Faith by Jacob of Edessa, Philoxenus of Mabūg, and the Maphrian Gregory; a brief sketch of sacred history, by Jacob of Edessa (ܐܓܪܬܐ ... ܥܠ ܡܕܒܪܢܘܬܐ ܕܐܠܗܐ ܕܒܪܝ ܫܘܪܝܐ ܘܫܪ̇); a tract on the Holy Eucharist, by Dionysius bar Ṣalībi; see also Or. 4403, fol. 30*a*. Paper, foll. 46. 8°. Different hands of the xviith Century.

Or. 2308. A treatise concerning the Children of Light, in seven ܦܘܣܩ̈ܐ, by Abu'l Ma'ānī (at the end, fol. 31*b*, ܫܠܡܬ ܬܫܥܝܬܐ ܕܐܒܘ ܐܠܡܥܐܢܝ ܘܫܪ̇).—An Epistle on the Holy Eucharist, by the same author. Both these works, apparently, also in Sachau's Verzeichniss, 198 (182). See the Oxford Catalogue of Syriac MSS., under "Aziz Bar-Sabto. . . . Ignatius VII., patriarcha Turabdensis."—Confessions of Faith, &c.—The MS. is imperfect. Paper, foll. 66. 8°. Dated (fol. 31*b*) A.GR. 1999 (A.D. 1688).

Or. 2309. Accounts of eleven Church-councils, beginning with the first Council of Nicaea, and ending with that of Florence: accompanied by extracts from the Annals of the Church of Rome. The contents of the MS. are identical with ܣܘܢܗܕܘܣ ܬܫܥܝܬܐ ܚܕܥܣ̈ܪܐ ܟܢܘ̈ܫܬܐ, published [by P. Bedjan] at Paris, in 1888. The Syriac translator was Joseph, Metropolitan of Amid. (See also Or. 4070.—Appended are (fol. 176 sqq.) an account of two Apostolic Councils, ordinances of individual Apostles, and the canons of a synod held by the Nestorian Church in the year 1629 of the Greeks (A.D. 1318).—Both parts of the MS. are imperfect. Paper, foll. 215. 8°. xviith Century.

Or. 2310. The Canons of the Council of Nicaea, followed by questions and answers on various theological subjects by Timothy ܬܐܘܠܘܓܐ ܦܛܪܝܪܟܗ ܕܡܕܢܚܐ (Timothy I.?), Theodore of Mopsuestia, and others. Papers, foll. 153. 8°. A.GR. 2068 (A.D. 1757).

Or. 2311. A large portion of the fourth part of the "Illustrations of the Book of Paradise" (probably composed by the monk 'Anān Yēshu'), beginning in the middle of section 46, and ending near the beginning of section 261. (See Wright's Catalogue, p. 1078, col. 2.) The writing is often blurred, and many leaves are damaged. Paper, foll. 168 (with two columns to a page). Large 8°. A bold regular hand of the xiith Century.

Or. 2312. The works of Isaiah of Scete (foll. 1—53*a*), and of Evagrius [Ponticus] (fol. 53*b* to the end). Both parts are fragmentary. Paper, foll. 182, with two columns to a page. 8°. A regular hand of the xvth—xvith Century.

Or. 2313. The Testimonies (ܣܗܕܘ̈ܬܐ) of the Prophets (Jeremiah, Daniel, Ezekiel, &c.), followed by a tract entitled ܟܬܒ ܒܪܘܢܝܐ ܠܘܬ ܐܠܗܝܢ ܕܐܡܪܝܢ ܗܝܡܢܘܬܐ ܕܠܐ ܠܡ ܙܪܝܪ ܠܫܠܝܚܘܬܗ ܕܦܘܠܘܣ ܫܠܝܚܐ, and other theological pieces. Imperfect.—Appended is a fragment of the story of Aḥīkar (fol. 172 sqq.); see also Or. 2326.—Paper, foll. 180. 12°. Nestorian writing of the xvith—xviith Century.

Or. 2314. The smaller Grammar of John bar Zō'bī. Imperfect. (See Wright's "Syriac Literature," p. 259.) Paper, foll. 164. 8°. Probably xvith Century.

Or. 2315. The Syro-Arabic Lexicon of Yēshū' bar 'Alī. Paper, foll. 202. Folio. xviith or xviiith Century.

Or. 2316. [ܬܫܥܝܬܐ ܘܬܘܪ̈ܥܬܐ ܡܘܬ̈ܪܢܝܬܐ ܕܥܠ ܐ̈ܢܫܐ ܩܕ̈ܝܫܐ ܘܝܚܝ̈ܕܝܐ ܕܗܘܘ ܒܕܪ ܕܪ ܒܥܘܡܪܐ ܩܕܝܫܐ ܕܒܝܬ ܥܒ̈ܐ ܕܣܝܡܝܢ ܠܩܕܝܫܐ ܡܪܝ ܬܐܘܡܐ ܐܦܝܣܩܘܦܐ ܕܡܪܓܐ] i.e. the histories and edifying (lit. useful, helpful) events of the holy men and monks who lived, generation after generation, in the holy monastery of Beth 'Ābhē, composed by the saintly Mār Thomas, Bishop of Margā. Imperfect. Published, with an English translation, by E. W. Budge, under the title of "The Book of Governors," in 1893. — A fragment (fol. 149) of an introduction to a history of martyrs, followed by a history of the martyrdom of Simeon bar Ṣabbā'ē and his companions (ܘܣܗܕܐ ܕܐܬܟܠܠܘ ܥܡܗ).—A history of Joseph, son of Jacob, ascribed to Basil of Cesaraea. Imperfect. See also Or. 4528. A portion of this work was published by Magnus Weinberg, from a Berlin MS., in 1893, and the rest by S. W. Link in 1895.—Paper, foll. 188. Folio. xviith—xviiith Century.

Or. 2317. A volume (imperfect at the beginning and end, and also having lacunae after foll. 2, 89, 121) containing a certain number of hymns and prayers for various occasions; an epistle of Mār Elias, Metropolitan of Nisibis, on حدث العالم ووحدانية الخالق . . . وتثليث الاقانيم[a] (fol. 39b); a paradigm of the Syriac verb ܐܙܠ, Arabic ذهب, in all its parts (fol. 11b); a divinatory tract, showing how to find out, by means of the letters ܐ — ܬ, whether

[a] See Assem., B. O., iii. 270: ii. 487.

a wish will be realized or not (fol. 85*b*); another divinatory tract, concerning one who has disappeared, a sick person, and a fugitive.—Nearly the whole of the MS. is in the Arabic language, but the character used is partly Syriac. Different hands of the xviiith Century, some portions being dated A.GR. 2017 (A.D. 1706) and A.GR. 2027 (A.D. 1716). Paper, foll. 127. 8°.

Or. 2318. The Ethics of Gregory Bar-Hebraeus, in Karshuni. Comp. Rosen and Forshall, Codices Syriaci, lv., and Zotenberg's Paris Catalogue of Syriac MSS., no. 247; also Sachau's Verzeichniss, 313 (2). See also Or. 4409. Paper, foll. 184. Large 8°. Dated A.GR. 1995 (A.D. 1684).

Or. 2319. A Jacobite Lectionary from the Gospels, with extracts from the exegetical works of John Chrysostom, Cyril of Alexandria, and other commentators. Karshuni. Paper, foll. 357. Folio. Dated A.GR. 2061 (A.D. 1750).

Or. 2320. ܟܬܐܒ ܐܠܡܪܫܕ, a work illustrative of the principles of the Christian Faith, according to the tenets of the Jacobite Church; composed by Abu Naṣr Yuḥanna (Yaḥya) ibn Ḥarīr, of Tagrit. The 31st chapter of this work (في الكهنة) has been edited by Dr. Cureton (issued by Wright in 1865) from a Bodleian MS., which also gives the fuller title of the work as كتاب المصباح المرشد الي الفلاح والنجاح الهادى من التيه الي سبيل النجاة, rendered into English by "The Lamp that guides to Salvation." See Ibn Abi Uṣaibiah, vol. i., p. 243, where the author is stated to have been alive A.H. 472 (A.D. 1079-80); cf. Assemani-Mai, Cat. Codd. Vat. (Scriptorum veterum nova collection, tom. 4, part 2), p. 212. Paper, foll. 224. Folio (two columns to a page). Dated A.GR. 2030 (A.D. 1719).

Or. 2321. Letters (in Karshuni) of Cyril of Alexandria (two to Nestorius, and one to ܐܣܩܦ ܣܘܩܣܘܣ ܩܝܣܪܝܗ ܐܠܕܝܘܩܝܣܪܝܗ, fol. 58*b*), and part of his Commentary on the Pentateuch (fol. 62*b*).—Homilies (also in Karshuni) of Athanasius, Patriarch of Jerusalem, Athanasius of Alexandria (one, fol. 39*b*), and ܐܬܢܐܣܝܘܣ, Patriarch of Antioch (one); see Assem. B. O., ii., pp. 302, 303. Paper, foll. 139. 8°. xviiith—xixth Century.

Or. 2322. A Karshuni work on Christian Ethics, in 36 chapters,[a] ascribed to Simeon, the Stylite, *junior* (?), of Antioch (ܣܡܥܢ ܐܠܥܡܘܕܝ ܐܠܥܓܐܝܒܝ ܐܠܐܢܛܐܟܝ), who was born A.D. 521 (see Smith's "Dictionary of Christian Biography," vol. iv., p. 681). The title-page begins: ܗܕܐ ܟܬܐܒ ܐܠܓܘܐܗܪ ܡܫܬܡܠ ܥܠܝ ܬܥܠܝܡ ܘܐܕܐܒ ܪܘܚܐܢܝܗ ܦܝ ܟܡܐܠ ܐܠܐܝܡܐܢ ܘܟܠ ܐܠܐܒܘܝܗ ܘܐܠܪܗܒܢܝܗ ܘܐܠܟܗܢܘܬܝܗ ܘܐܠܢܣܟܝܗ. Comp. Assemani-Mai, tom. iv., p. 182, where a work in 20 chapters, covering part of the contents of this MS., is described. Paper, foll. 199. 8°. xviiith Century.

Or. 2323. A volume of Sermons, in Karshuni, by Ignatius Shukrullah, Patriarch of Antioch in the latter half of the xviith Century, or another of about A.D. 1730 (see Wright's Syr. Cat., p. 900, col. 2; Rosen and Forshall, p. 109, col. 1). Paper, foll. 202. 8°. Dated A.GR. 2112 (A.D. 1801).

Or. 2324. تسهيل المنافع في الطب الخ, a medical work by Ibrāhīm ibn 'Abd al-Raḥmān.—A work, in 35 chapters,

[a] Another copy is Or. 4092 (p. 29).

treating on ܟܠܡܬ ܐܠܐܠܗܝܗ ܘܐܠܐܠܟܝܢ ܘܐܠܐܠܗܝܢ ܘܐܠܪܝܐܨܝܐܬ ܘܐܠܛܒܝܥܝܐܬ, ascribed to Jacob of Edessa (fol. 128*b*).—Two astronomical treatises (ܟܬܐܒ ܐܠܢܓܘܡ, in 60 chapters, fol. 197*a*, and (?) ܟܬܐܒ ܢܘܗ̈ ܐܠܢܓܘܡ ܦܝ ܐܠܡܒܬܕܐ ܐܠܠܠ ܘܐܠܕܗܪ, a compendium of the ܟܬܐܒ ܐܠܕܗܪܝ ܘܐܠܕܗܪ ܒܐܠܢܓܘܡ, fol. 241*a*).—All these works are in Karshuni, though the title of the first is in the Arabic character. Paper, foll. 260. 8°. Written in two different hands, the second portion being dated A.GR. 2110 (A.D. 1799).

Or. 2325. ܟܬܐܒ ܡܥܒܪܗ̈ ܐܣܪܐܪ ܐܠܟܗܢܘܬ̈, a Karshuni theological treatise in eight *Maḳālāt*, composed by Mār Basilius, i.e. the Maphrian Shimeon al-Ṭurānī (ܡܦܪܝܢܐ ܫܡܥܘܢ ܐܠܡܥܪܘܦ ܐܠܛܘܪܐܢܝ). See also Or. 4426. Paper, foll. 138. Dated A.GR. 2111 (A.D. 1800).

Or. 2326. A Karshuni collection of works in the following order:—The "Natural History" known by the title of "Physiologus" (imperfect at the end). Homily of St. Chrysostom on Repentance (fol. 51*a*).—The concluding lines (fol. 65*a*) of a tract entitled مناجات موسى, written in the Arabic character, the Karshuni copy being preserved in Add. 7209, fol. 213*b* sqq. See Rosen and Forshall, Codices Carshunice, p. 111.—The story of Ḥaikar or Aḥiḳar (fol. 65*b*; imperfect); compare the Syriac fragment contained in Or. 2313, foll. 172—180.—Story of the Picture of Christ revealed to the deacon Philippus.—Paper, foll. 105. 8°. Written in different hands, the first-named work belonging to the xixth, and the rest to the xvith Century.

Or. 2327. Revelation of St. Gregory [Thaumaturgus?] concerning punishments in the future life (ܐܒܬܕܐܦ ܐܠܩܕܝܣ ܡܐܪ ܓܪܝܓܘܪܝܘܣ).—Miracles of the Virgin Mary.—Both works are in Karshuni. Fragmentary. Paper, foll. 83. 8°. Dated (fol. 8*a*) A.GR. 1969 (A.D. 1658).

Or. 2343. The Marriage Services of the Nestorian Church. Imperfect. Written on paper, in a Nestorian hand of the xviiith Century.—A Manual of Confession, in Karshuni, translated, or adapted, from a Latin work, by Germanus Farḥāt, the Maronite Bishop of Aleppo (ܒܕ ܠܐܢܒܐ ܓܪܡܐܢܘܣ ܦܪܚܐܬ ܐܠܡܪܘܢܝ. ܐܠܠܒܢܐܢܝ ܐܣܩܦ ܚܠܒ ܡܢ ܪܐܝ ܟܬܒ ܟܠܡܐ ܐܠܡܣܝܚܝܗ ܐܠܡܥܪܘܦܝܗ). A life and portrait of Germanus Farḥāt are prefixed to the edition of his dictionary (باب الاعراب).— European paper. xixth Century. The volume contains 125 leaves in all. 8°.

Or. 2440. A large fragment of a Jacobite Lectionary from the Gospels, the text being mainly taken from the Ḥarklensian version. Vellum, foll. 126. 8°. xiith Century.

Or. 2441. The Syriaco-Arabic Lexicon of Ḥasan bar Bahlūl. Paper, foll. 400. Folio. Dated A.D. 1878.

Or. 2442. A Karshuni version of the Fables of Aesop, bearing the title: ܢܙܗܗ ܐܠܢܦܘܣ ܘܡܦܟܗܗ ܡܢ ܐܠܚܟܝܡ ܠܘܩܡܐܢ. See pp. 8, 9, 20 sqq. in "Beiträge zur Syrischen Fabelliteratur" of S. Hochfeld (1893). Paper, foll. 82. 8°. Badly written. xviiith—xixth Century.

Or. 2450. Hortatory compositions, in heptasyllabic

metre, on Christian life, character, and duties, composed by a monk whose name is not given. Some noteworthy parts of the collection are versified renderings of portions of the Proverbs, Ecclesiastes, and Ecclesiasticus.—Other pieces are exhortations (ܦܘܩܕ̈ܢܐ ܘܙܘܗܪ̈ܐ, fol. 160*b*) by John, a monk of the convent of St. Michael at Mosul; a similar piece by ܡܒܝܢ ܕܝ ܦܝܕܝܟܐ (fol. 168*b*); and two stories of saints. Paper, foll. 180. 4°. Dated Teshrin, A.GR. 1882 (A.D. 1570).

Or. 2695. The Canon of the New Testament as accepted by the early Syrian Church, viz. the four Gospels; the Acts of the Apostles; the Catholic Epistles (James, 1 Peter, 1 John); the Epistles of St. Paul (including the Epistle to the Hebrews). At the end: ܫܪ̈ܒܐ ܡܫܘܕܪ̈ܐ ܕܩܪܝܢ ܐܘܢܓܠܝܘܢ ܘܦܪ̈ܟܣܐ ܕܐܫܠܝܚ̈ܐ ܠܗ ܟܠ ܕܩܘܪ̈ܝܢܬܗܘܢ ܘܟܠ ܟܪ̈ܘܙܘܬܗܘܢ ܘܡܫܘܕܥܘܬܗܘܢ ܕܫܠܝ̈ܚܐ ܩܕ̈ܝܫܐ. Vellum, foll. 249. Sm. folio. Dated A.GR. 1514 =A.H. 599 (A.D. 1202-3). A painted cross on fol. 248*a*.

Or. 2732. A volume containing the Canticles or Biblical Hymns; prayers by Philoxenos of Mabūg, Isaiah of Scete, Isaac of Niniweh, Ephrem Syrus, and others; history of Marcus the Monk (ܕܡܪܩܘܣ ܗܘܐ ܒܛܘܪܐ ܕܬܪܡܩܐ; see Amélineau, Contes et Romans de l'Égypte Chrétienne, p. 55 sqq.; also see Wright's Cat. Index under "Mark, the Monk"; also Or. 1272); discourses of Ephrem Syrus, Isaac of Antioch, Jacob of Serūg, and others. These works, which are all in Syriac, are followed (fol. 164*a* sqq.) by prayers in Karshuni.—Paper, foll. 177. 12°. xviiith Century.

Or. 3311. A volume containing the following two Karshuni works:—1. ܐܟܒܐܪ ܐܠܩܕܝܣܝܢ, i.e. Stories of Saints, embracing the lives of ܝܘܚܢܐ ܐܠܪܚܘܡ ܪܐܣ ܐܣܐܩܦܗ ܐܠܐܣܟܢܕܪܝܗ (Joannes Eleemosynarius), by Leontius, Bishop of Neapolis in Cyprus (see Wright's Cat., p. 1113, col. 1), of ܝܘܣܒܐ and other saints (fol. 44*b*), and of John of the Golden Gospel (fol. 58*a*).—2. (fol. 71*a*) ܡܘܥܙܗ ܥܠܝ ܐܠܬܠܐܬܗ ܐܩܐܢܝܡ ܐܠܐܠܗ ܐܠܘܐܚܕ ܦܝ ܟܠ ܐܠܟܢܐܝܣ ܘܗܝ ܡܟܬܘܒܗ ܡܢ ܐܠܟܬܐܒ ܐܠܡܩܕܣܗ : ܡܢ ܩܘܠ ܐܠܡܥܠܡ ܐܠܝܐܣ ܐܠܟܒܝܪ ܪܒܢܐ ܝܥܩܘܒ ܐܒܢ .. ܥܝܣܘ ܐܠܡܠܦܢܪ.—Paper, foll. 131. 8°. Dated A.GR. 1849 (A.D. 1538).

Or. 3335. ܟܬܒܐ ܕܨܡܚܐ, i.e. "Liber Splendorum," the larger Grammar of the Syriac language by Gregory Bar-Hebraeus. Paper, foll. 353. Sm. 8°. Dated A.GR. 1643=A.H. 733 (A.D. 1332).

Or. 3336. Five discourses (ܡܐܡܪܐ) on the Services of the Church for week-days and Sundays, by Gabriel Ḳaṭraya (the same writer whose works are recorded by 'Ebed-Yēshū' ?; see Assemani, Bibliotheca Orientalis, vol. iii., pp. 172-3. The autograph of an earlier Gabriel Ḳaṭraya (A.D. 615) is found in the Brit. Mus. MS. Add. 14,471; see Wright's Syriac Catalogue, p. 53, col. 2). Paper, foll. 230. Sm. 4°. Dated A.GR. 1579 (A.D. 1268).

Or. 3337. A volume of miscellaneous contents, consisting chiefly of lives of saints, epistles, and liturgical portions. Among the pieces contained in the collection are an account of saints who lived in the time of Jeremiah the Prophet; the story of the repentant demons (ܬܝܒܘܬܐ ܕܫܐܕܐ ܬܝܒܐ ... ܐܡܪܘ .. ܩܘܡ

ܬܫܥܝܬܐ ܕܣܘܠܦܝܢ ܡܬܩܪ̈ܝܢ܀ (ܘܐܦܠܘ ܘܐܪܦܠܝܡܘܣ); ܘܡܠܠ ܬܘܪ̈ܥܐ; ܘܡܠܠ ܬܘܪ̈ܥܐ ܕܒܡܣܘܣ of John, Metropolitan of Arbel; ܐܓܪ̈ܬܐ ܕܡܪܝ܀ ܡܫܪ ܝܫܘܥ ܕܦܠܘܣ ܕܡܝܬ; ܠܡܪܝܢ ܕܐܬܘܬܗܘܢ ܒܪ ܡܫܝܚܐ; ܘ ܡܐܡܪ̈ܐ of Yēshū'-yahb, Metropolitan of Arbel. Paper, foll. 310. Sm. 8°. Dated (fol. 251*a*) A.GR. 1834 (A.D. 1523).

Or. 3372. A Jacobite Lectionary (Philoxenian version, with Greek readings in the margin) from the Gospels, for the whole year. Imperfect at the end.—Prefixed are a table of lessons, and five miniatures executed in gold and colours, representing the Cross, the birth and baptism of Christ, His entry into Jerusalem, and the four Evangelists. There are also ornamental designs at the beginning of the sections. Vellum. Folio. Probably of the xiith Century. Dr. J. Lee's (?) bookplate at the end. (See Dr. J. Lee's "Oriental Manuscripts, purchased in Turkey," p. 22, no. 113; 2nd edition, p. 3, no. 6).

Or. 3636. ܬܫܥܝܬܐ ... ܕܡܪܝ ܝܗܒܐܠܗܐ ... ܘܪܒܢ ܨܘܡܐ, the Lives of Mār Yahb-alāhā and of Rabban Ṣauma. See the printed text. Paper, foll. 70. 4°. xixth Century.

Or. 3652. The ܟܬܒܐ ܕܣܘܕ ܣܘܦܝܐ, a compendium of Dialectics, Physics, and Metaphysics or Theology, by Gregory Bar-Hebraeus. Syriac and Arabic in parallel columns. Imperfect at the beginning and the end. Paper, foll. 33. Sm. 8°. Finely written. Probably of the xvth Century.

Or. 4051. The New Testament, viz. the four Gospels, the Acts of the Apostles, the three Catholic Epistles of the early Syrian Church, and the Pauline Epistles, according to the Peshitta version. Imperfect at the beginning. Written in the xiiith Century, and restored in the xviiith. Paper, foll. 276. 4°.

Or. 4052. A fragment of the Gospel of St. Matthew, and the greater part of the Gospels of St. Mark and St. Luke, according to the Peshitta version; divided into lessons throughout. Paper, foll. 99. Sm. 4°. xiiith—xivth Century.

Or. 4053. The Psalms, according to the Peshitta version, divided into sections styled ܗܘ̈ܠܠܐ and ܡܪ̈ܡܝܬܐ, with short arguments ascribed to Theodore of Mopsuestia.—The Canticles, or Biblical hymns, viz. the first Song of Moses, the Song of Isaiah, and the second and third Songs of Moses.—Hymns and Prayers for various occasions.—ܬܘܪ̈ܓܡܐ, or "conciones" for the Eucharist.—Hymns (ܩܠ̈ܐ), twelve in number, addressed to the martyrs, for the evening and morning of each week day; see also Or. 4059.—Paper, foll. 178. 4°. Dated A.GR. 2113 (A.D. 1802).

Or. 4054. The Psalms, according to the Peshitta version, with a Karshuni translation in parallel columns; divided into fifteen ܡܪ̈ܡܝܬܐ, with Ps. cli. (ܠܒܪ ܡܢ ܡܢܝܢܐ) at the end.—The Canticles, or Biblical hymns, the Nicene Creed, &c., also in Syriac and Karshuni (fol. 211*b*).—ܡܐܡܪܐ ܕܫܘܡܠܝܐ, a metrical discourse, in rhymed pairs, on Perfection, by Gregory Bar-Hebraeus.—Paper, foll. 240. 4°. xviiith Century.

Or. 4055. The Psalms, divided into twenty Cathismata (according to the use of the Greek Church), followed by the Canticles, or Biblical hymns. Karshuni. Paper, foll. 137. Sm. 8°. Dated A.GR. 1959 (A.D. 1648).

Or. 4056. A Jacobite Lectionary for the whole year, from the Gospels, according to the Peshiṭta, and partly according to the Ḥarklensian version. Paper, foll. 186. Folio. Dated A.D. 1788.

Or. 4057. ܒܥܘܬܐ ܕܢܝܢܘܝܐ, or "Prayer of the Ninivites," Nestorian Services in commemoration of the three days' fast of the Ninivites. Imperfect at the end. Vellum, foll. 142. 4°. xiiith Century.

Or. 4058. Another copy of the ܒܥܘܬܐ ܕܢܝܢܘܝܐ, with headings in coloured ornamental characters and various coloured designs. Imperfect. Paper, foll. 106. Long 8°. Fine Nestorian hand of the xiiith Century.

Or. 4059. I. ܛܟܣܐ ܕܩܕܡ ܘܕܒܬܪ, or "The Order of the Before and After," a Nestorian Service-book (see Badger, "The Nestorians and their Rituals," ii., p. 23). —A series of twelve Hymns (ܡܠܐ) addressed to the martyrs, for the evening and morning of the ferial days of the week; see also Or. 4053.—A series of hymns styled ܒܥܘܬܐ ܕܛܘܒܗ ܝܪ̈ܚܐ, invoking prosperity for the months of the year. This part is dated A.GR. 2130 (A.D. 1819).—II. A Nestorian Service-book containing the Offices of Ordination of Readers, Sub-deacons, Deacons, and Presbyters; also the Offices for the consecration of the altar and the Eucharistic vessels, and a shorter form of the above-mentioned Offices of Ordination. Dated 1885.—Paper, foll. 164. 4°.

Or. 4060. A Nestorian Sacerdotal, or Priest's Office-book, containing, among other pieces, fragments of several Liturgies (ܩܘܕܫܐ); ܩܘܕܫ ܡܪ̈ܝܐ ܠܫܠܝ̈ܚܐ; ܛܟܣܐ ܕܚܘܕܬ ܡܕܒܚܐ; ܛܟܣܐ ܕܩܘܕܫ ܡܥܡܕܢܐ ܕܠܐ ܡܫܚܐ; the ܐܒܘܣܠܡ, i.e. a collection of prayers for the feasts, by the Catholicos Mār Elias III.; ܚܘܬܡܐ, or dismissory hymns; ܛܟܣܐ ܕܦܘܠܓܬܐ ܕܡܬܒܥܝܢ ܕܒܥܡܝܢ ܕܦܩܘܣܝܐ. The MS. is very fragmentary throughout. Paper, foll. 74. Sm. 4º. xvith Century.

Or. 4061. Another Chaldaean (Romanist) Sacerdotal, containing (1) a Lectionary, for the days of the week, from the Pauline Epistles and the Gospels; (2) the Liturgy of the Apostles[a]; (3) Canons for the feasts (partly with a Karshuni translation in parallel columns); (4) ܚܘܬܡܐ, or dismissory hymns (on fol. 58*b*: ܚܘܬܡ̈ܐ ܐܫܢ̈ܝܐ ܕܟܗܢܝܢ ܠܟܗܢ̈ܐ ܡܫܒܚ ܕܦܪ̈ܢܓܝܐ ܕܟܠܕܝܐ); (5) ܛܟܣܐ ܕܫܝܓܬܐ ܕܪ̈ܓܠܐ, or the Office of the washing of the feet; ܛܟܣܐ ܕܥܡܕܐ ܩܕܝܫܐ, the Office of Holy Baptism; (6) ܛܟܣܐ ܕܩܘܕܫ ܡܝ̈ܐ ܐܝܟ ܥܝܕܐ ܕܥܕܬܐ ܩܕܝܫܬܐ ܩܬܘܠܝܩܝ ܕܪܗܘܡܐ, the Office of the consecration of water according to the use of the Holy Catholic Church of Rome; (7) Prayers and benedictions, chiefly for women; (8) ܚܪܡܐ ܕܡܬܝܗܒܐ ܘܫܠܡܐ ܕܗܘܘ ܡܬܦܣܩܝܢ ܚܪܡܐ ܕܠܐ ܚܪܡܐ ܘܚܪܡܐ ܕܠܗܘܢ, and similar Offices for the removal of the ban of excommunication; (9) Offices for the sick and dying; (10) Office of complete absolution (ܡܫܒܩܢܘܬܐ ܫܘܡܠܝܐ ܠܡܝܬܐ), which was administered at the time of death to all Christians who had helped to put down idolatry and heresy; (11) a similar Office of absolution administered ܠܡܫܒܩܘܬܗ

[a] Mār Addai and Mār Mārī.

ܒܠܫܢܐ ܕܠܒܘܫ. ܒܬܘܠܬܐ ܡܪܝܡ ܕܐܪܬܘܕܘܟܣܘ ܣܘܡܩܐ ܠܚܕܪܐ.—Paper, foll. 129. 8°. Dated A.GR. 2162= A.D. 1851.

Or. 4062. A large collection of Hymns (ܥܘܢ̈ܝܬܐ) by Gabriel Ḳamṣā, Metropolitan of Mosul; Khamīs bar Ḳardāḥē; Gīorgīs Warda; Rabban Mārī bar Mĕshīḥā; the priest Ṣĕlībā bar David; Yĕshū'-yahb, Metropolitan of Arbel; and the priest Isaac ܡܪܕܝܐ ܫܒܕܢܝܐ. Coloured ornamental designs at the beginning of different sections. Imperfect. Paper, foll. 143. Sm. folio. Dated A.GR. 1985 (A.D. 1674), restored A.GR. 2010 (A.D. 1699).

Or. 4063. A similar collection of Hymns (ܥܘܢ̈ܝܬܐ) by Gabriel Ḳamṣā, Metropolitan of Mosul; Khamīs bar Ḳardāḥē; Gīorgīs Warda; Rabban Mārī bar Mĕshīḥā; the priest Ṣĕlība bar David; Yēshū'-yahb, Metropolitan of Arbel; the priest Isaac ܡܪܕܝܐ ܫܒܕܢܝܐ; the priest 'Aṭāyē bar Āteli; 'Ebed-Yēshū' of Gāzartā Zabdaitā; and the priest Israel of Alkōsh. Imperfect at the end. Paper, foll. 231. Folio. xviiith Century.

Or. 4064. Choral Services for Compline (ܣܘܬܪ̈ܐ) of the days of the week, including a ܣܕܪܐ by Ephrem Syrus, and ܒܥܘܬ̈ܐ by Ephrem and Jacob of Serūg. Paper, foll. 54. Sm. 8°. xixth Century.

Or. 4065. Prayers for the seven daily canonical hours, by Philoxenus of Mabūg, Serapion, Paul the Simple, Abraham Ḳīdūnāyā, Isaiah of Scete, Isaac of Niniweh, and others: accompanied by the Psalms proper for each Service.—Praises of Mary, the Mother of God.—A collection of divers prayers, with some by Basil the Great and John Chrysostom at the end.—The last-named part is in Karshuni, the rest in Syriac.

Paper, foll. 203. Sm. 8°. Dated (fol. 81*a*) A.GR. 2032 (A.D. 1721).

Or. 4066. A small volume (imperfect at the beginning and the end), opening with prayers and adjurations uttered by the Blessed Virgin Mary, and also containing, among other portions, a prayer of Mār Cyprianus, and a hymn of Mār Elias, Metropolitan of Nisibis. The contents are mainly in Karshuni. Paper, foll. 37. 12°. xviiith Century.

Or. 4067. Nestorian Funeral Services for all ranks, consisting of ten ܡܘܬܒ̈ܐ, or Sessions; ܩܪ̈ܝܢܐ, or Lessons from the Old and New Testaments; ܬܘܪ̈ܓܡܐ, or Conciones; and ܩ̈ܠܐ, or Hymns. Imperfect at the beginning and end. Paper, foll. 178. 4°. xvth Century.

Or. 4068. ܟܬܒܐ ܕܦܪܕܝܣܐ ܕܥܕܢ, a collection of fifty Poems on theological subjects, by 'Ebed-Yēshū', Metropolitan of Nisibis and Armenia. Paper, foll. 94. Sm. folio. xviith Century.

Or. 4069. A collection of works by 'Ebed-Yēshū', Metropolitan of Nisibis and Armenia, viz. (1) ܟܬܒܐ ܕܦܪܕܝܣܐ ܕܥܕܢ; (2) ܟܬܒܐ ܕܡܪܓܢܝܬܐ, or "The Book of the Pearl," a theological work in five sections; (3) The well-known Catalogue of Syriac books (ܡܐܡܪܐ ܕܐܝܬ ܒܗ ܡܢܝܢܐ ܕܟܠܗܘܢ ܟܬܒ̈ܐ ܥܕܬܢܝ̈ܐ); (4) Discourse on the computation of time (ܡܐܡܪܐ ܕܥܒܕ ܥܠܗ ܚܘܫܒܢܐ ܕܩܪܘܢܝܩܘܢ), composed in dodecasyllabic metre. The first three works are not wholly perfect. At the end (fol. 122*a* sqq.): (5) ܥܠܬ ܡܢ ܟܬܒܐ ܕܐܘܢܓܠܝܘܢ ܐܠܗܝܐ, by the same author, enumerating the principal events in the life of our Lord. Dated A.GR. 2033 (A.D. 1722); restored A.GR. 2067 (A.D. 1756), and in the present century. Paper, foll. 123. Folio.

Or. 4070. ܠܡܕܒܪܐ ܢܘܗܪܐ, or ܕܣܘܢܗܕܘܣ ܟܬܒܐ (both titles on fol. 191*a*), accounts of eleven Church Councils, beginning with the first Council of Nicaea, and ending with that of Florence. These are accompanied by extracts from the Annals of the Church of Rome. The work was originally translated from the Latin into Arabic, and afterwards from the Arabic into Syriac, by Joseph, Metropolitan of Amid, whose introductions are prefixed to the accounts of the Synods. See also Or. 2309, and Bedjan's edition (Paris, 1888). Paper, foll. 192. 8°. Dated A.D. 1823 = A.GR. 2134.

Or. 4071. Canons of the Apostles; imperfect at the beginning.—Fragment of a work, in heptasyllabic metre, on words (alphabetically arranged) which are similar in spelling but different in meaning, by Mār 'Ebed-Yēshū' of Gāzartā (fol. 24*a*, Hoffmann, Opuscula Nestoriana, p. 49 sqq.).—Explanations of the different words in the preceding work, wanting a few lines at the beginning (fol. 31*a*, Hoffm., Opusc. Nest., p. 70 sqq.).—ܐܘܚܕܬܐ, or Enigmas (fol. 38*b*).—ܫܘܐܠܐ ܕܒܥܝܢ ܠܗ ܟܕ ܠܗ ܠܣܦܪ̈ ܡܫܐܠ ܫܘܐܠܐ[*] ܟܠ ܗܘ ܕܡܬܘܪܐ ܒܪܢܫܐ ܟܠܡܐ ܘܒܪܘܪܐ (fol. 45*b*).—A metrical discourse of Mār Isaac (of Antioch), profitable for solitaries (ܕܝܚܝܕ ܠܝܚܝܕܝܐ ܕܗܘܝܢ ܡܥܠܝܐ, fol. 59*b*).—Recipes for eye-salves (fol. 65*a*).—ܡܐܡܪܐ ܕܥܠ ܦܝܠܣܘܦܘܬܐ ܘܕܘܒܪܬܐ ܕܡܠܟܘܬ

* See Hoffmann, Opuscula Nestoriana, p. xxi.; also Cambridge Add. MS. 2812. fol. 29*a*.

ܐܠܗܘܬܐ (fol. 66*b*).—Fragment of a dictionary on synonymous terms (fol. 79*a*).—Another lexicographical fragment (fol. 82*a*).—Poems by Khamīs (fol. 91*a*). Discourse on the soul, entitled "The Bird" (ܦܪܚܬܐ), in dodecasyllabic metre, by the Patriarch John (or Aaron) bar Ma'dani (fol. 96*a*), followed by another metrical discourse of the same author on the "Way of the Perfect" (ܐܘܪܚܐ ܕܓܡܝܪ̈ܐ).—ܡܐܡܪ̈ܐ ܥܘܢܝ̈ܬܐ, a metrical discourse, in rhymed pairs, on Divine things and on Perfection, by Gregory Bar-Hebraeus, with the additions of Khamīs bar Ḳardāḥē and Yēshū'-yabh, Metropolitan of Arbel (fol. 107*b*); imperfect at the end.—Paper, foll. 150. 8°. Dated A.GR. 1991 (A.D. 1680).

Or. 4072. The fourth volume of the Homilies of the priest Emmanuel bar Shahhārē on the Hexaemeron, or six days of Creation (originally 28 in number, but the first three are here wanting), composed partly in heptasyllabic, partly in dodecasyllabic metre. See also Or. 1300. Paper, foll. 303. Sm. 4°. xvith Century.

Or. 4073. ܟܬܒܐ ܕܗܒܠܐ ܕܥܠܡܐ, or "Book of the Vanities of the World," an ethical work in 51 sections, translated from the Spanish of Padre ܕܝܓܘܕܐܣܛܝܠܐ[a] into Arabic by Padre Rūfā'ēl, and from Arabic into Syriac by the Presbyter ܚܢܐ of Mosul, A.D. 1724 =A.GR. 2035. Paper, foll. 226. 8°. Dated A.GR. 2114= A.D. 1804.

Or. 4074. The works (Epistles and Discourses) of John Sābā (on fol. 117*b*: (?) ܕܡܬܘܪܐ ܕܕܠܝܬܗ; see Wright's

[a] *I.e.* Didacus de Estella; see Antonio, Bibliotheca Nova, i., p. 283.

"Syriac Literature," p. 109). Imperfect. Paper, foll. 119. Sm. 4°. xvth Century.

Or. 4075. A volume containing 24 metrical discourses of Isaac of Antioch. The first treats ܥܠ ܦܘܠܚܢܐ, and the last is a ܡܐܡܪܐ ܕܬܝܒܘܬܐ. This collection should be compared with that given in Assemani, Bibliotheca Orientalis, i. 214 sqq., and the discourses enumerated in Wright's Catalogue and elsewhere. Paper, foll. 198. Sm. 4°. xviiith Century.

Or. 4076. The same collection of metrical discourses by Isaac of Antioch as is contained in the preceding number, though attributed to Isaac of Niniweh in a colophon at the end of the present MS. Paper, foll. 157. Sm. 4°. xviith Century; restored xviiith—xixth Century. The date (fol. 157*b*) A.GR. 1999 (A.D. 1688) probably belonged to the MS. from which the more modern portion was copied.

Or. 4077. [a]ܟܬܒܐ ܕܕܘܪ̈ܫܐ, Discourses on Theological subjects, composed in heptasyllabic metre, and divided into three parts (each part being called ܦܠܓܘܬܐ), by Elias, Bishop of Pērōz-Shābhōr or al-Anbar. The first part is missing entirely, and the two extant parts are defective. Paper, foll. 246. Folio. xviith Century.

Or. 4078. A copy of the "History of Joseph," consisting of discourses, in heptasyllabic metre, that had been attributed to St. Ephrem Syrus, but are now held to have been written by Balaeus. See the printed editions. Paper, foll. 141. 8°. xixth Century.

Or. 4079. ܚܐܘܬ ܚܟܡܬܐ, "Butyrum Sapientiae," or

[a] The same as Or. 4419, where see references; also contained in Cambridge Add. MS. 1995.

ܚܐܘܬ ܚ̈ܟܡܬܐ, "Butyrum Sapientiarum" (less correctly: ܚܟܡܬ ܚ̈ܟܡܬܐ, or "Sapientia Sapientiarum"), a compendium of the whole Aristotelian discipline, in three parts, by Gregory Bar-Hebraeus. Part I. contains the Logic, viz. the Isagōgē, Categories, De Interpretatione, Prior and Posterior Analytics, Dialectics, De Sophisticis Elenchis, Rhetoric, and Art of Poetry.[a] Part II. comprises the Physics, viz. De Ausculatione Physica, De Coelo et Mundo, De Generatione et Corruptione, De Fossilibus, De Meteoris, De Plantis, De Animalibus, and De Anima. Part III. treats on Metaphysics, viz. Philosophy and Theology, and on Ethics, Economics, and Politics. Paper, foll. 322. Large folio. Dated A.GR. 2120 = A.D. 1809.—Foll. 316—322 contain an incomplete table of contents on small quarto paper leaves.

Or. 4080. ܬܐܓܪܬ ܬܐܓܖ̈ܬܐ, or "Mercatura Mercaturarum," an abridgment (by the author himself) of the ܚܐܘܬ ܚ̈ܟܡܬܐ of Gregory Bar-Hebraeus. Paper, foll. 118. Sm. 4°. xvth Century.

Or. 4081. ܟܬܒܐ ܕܗܘܕܝܐ, or "Book of Directions," the Nomocanon of Gregory Bar-Hebraeus, to which is appended a list of the author's works. Paper, foll. 168. Folio. Dated A.D. 1887.

Or. 4082. ܟܬܒܐ ܕܐܝܬܝܩܘܢ, the Ethics of Gregory Bar-Hebraeus, in four books, with index prefixed. Paper, foll. 205. Folio. Dated A.GR. 2194 = A.D. 1883.—Fol. 205 is a fragment of a much earlier copy of this work.

Or. 4083. ܐܘܨܪ ܐܖ̈ܙܐ, or "Storehouse of Secrets,"

[a] The Poetica was printed by Prof. D. S. Margoliouth, Analecta Orientalia ad Poetic. Aristot., pp. ١١٤ ١٤١. For other MSS. of the whole, see Wright's Syr. Lit., p. 270.

a Commentary on the Old and New Testaments, by Gregory Bar-Hebraeus, viz. Pentateuch (fol. 1*b*), Chronological tables (fol. 72*b*), Joshua (fol. 75*a*), Judges (fol. 79*b*), Samuel (fol. 86*a*), Chronological tables (fol. 101*a*), Psalms (fol. 102*b*), Kings (fol. 174*a*), Chronological tables (fol. 192*a*), Proverbs (fol. 193*b*), Bar-Sira, i.e. Ecclesiasticus (fol. 197*a*), Ecclesiastes (fol. 200*b*), Song of Songs (fol. 203*a*), Wisdom (fol. 206*b*), Ruth (fol. 207*b*), Job (fol. 208*b*), Isaiah (fol. 214*b*), Minor Prophets (fol. 226*a*), Jeremiah (fol. 238*a*), Ezekiel (fol. 243*a*), Daniel (fol. 250*a*), Chronological tables (fol. 256*b*).—The four Gospels (fol. 259*b*), Acts of the Apostles (fol. 335*b*), the three Catholic Epistles of the early Syrian Church (fol. 346*a*), the fourteen Epistles of St. Paul (fol. 349*a*).—Paper, foll. 373. Folio. Dated A.D. 1884—7.

Or. 4084. ܡܐܡܪܐ ܕܫܘܠܡܐ, a metrical discourse, in rhymed pairs, on Divine things and on Perfection, by Gregory Bar-Hebraeus, with the additions of Khamīs bar Ḳardāḥē; Yēshū‘-yahb, Metropolitan of Arbel (composed A.GR. 1763 = A.D. 1452); and Joseph II., Patriarch of the Chaldeans, of Tell-Kēfē (composed A.GR. 2009 = A.D. 1698). Paper, foll. 82. 8°. Dated A.D. 1871 = A.GR. 2182.

Or. 4085. The same work as the preceding, also having the additions of the three writers there mentioned, together with those of a fourth author; imperfect at the beginning.—ܥܢܝܢܐ, or Hymns.—Fragments of the Syriac Grammars of Elias of Nisibis and (the longer work of) John bar Zō‘bī. Paper, foll. 130. 4°. xviith Century.

Or. 4086. ܟܬܒܐ ܕܣܘܕ ܣܘܦܝܐ, or "Book of the Speech of Wisdom," a compendium of Dialectics, Physics, and Metaphysics or Theology, by Gregory Bar-Hebraeus.—ܟܬܒܐ ܕܝܘܢܐ, or "Book of the Dove," a manual for ascetics, by the same author (fol. 33*b*), recently edited by G. Cardahi (Rome), together with a recension of the next piece. — Story relating to the childhood of Bar-Hebraeus, composed by himself (fol. 75*b*).—Grammar in four parts (ܡܐܡܪ̈ܐ) by the Presbyter Samuel Jamīl, of Tell-Kēfē (fol. 78*b*).—Metrical treatise on the punctuation (ܡܫܘܚܬܐ ܕܢܘܩܙܐ), by Joseph (or Yēshū'-yabh) bar Malkon, Bishop of Mārdīn (fol. 129*b*, see Wright's "Syriac Literature," pp. 256-7). — Metrical Grammar of John bar Zō'bī (fol. 145*b*, see Wright's Cat., p. 117, col. 1). — Metrical tract, by the same, on ܢܘܩܙܐ ܕܒ̈ܢܝܢܐ (fol. 158*a*, Wright's Cat., ibid.). — Metrical enumeration of the inflections (fol. 158*b*). — On the vowel-points Zelāmā ḳashya and Zĕlāma pĕshīḳa (fol. 159*a*).—Poem on the letters of the alphabet, in heptasyllabic metre, by Khamīs (fol. 159*b*).—Paper, foll. 166. Sm. 4°. Dated A.D. 1806.

Or. 4087. ܟܬܒܐ ܕܣܘܕ ܣܘܦܝܐ, or "Book of the Speech of Wisdom," by Gregory Bar-Hebraeus, in Syriac and Karshuni.—Question of Khamīs, the Nestorian, addressed to Rabban Daniel bar Ḥaṭṭāb (ܚܛܐܒ, but probably for خطّاب), with the answer of the latter and the fuller answer of Gregory Bar-Hebraeus. — Metrical epistle of Denḥā, Catholicus of the Nestorians, in reply to Gregory Bar-Hebraeus. — Three metrical discourses of Gregory Bar-Hebraeus, viz. (1) on Divine Love, (2) on the admirable constitution of the Heavens (ܥܠ ܬܫܡܫܬ ܬܘܡܢܐ ܕܫܡܝܐ), (3) on the decease of the Patriarch John bar Ma'dani. — Two metrical discourses of John bar Ma'dani, viz. (1) on the Soul, and (2) on the Way of the Perfect.—Paper, foll. 98. Sm. 4°. Dated A.GR. 1959 (A.D. 1648).

Or. 4088. The metrical Grammar of Gregory Bar-Hebraeus, including Section V. (De Vocibus Aequivocis); accompanied by the Scholia (see Martin, Oeuvres Grammaticales d'Abou 'l-Faradj, &c., tome ii.; for the other Museum copies see the Catalogues of Rosen and Forshall and Wright). — Appended is the poem beginning ܐܬܐܡܪ ܠܐܪܣܛܘܛܠܝܣ (see the edition of S. Samuel, Halle A.S., 1893).—Paper, foll. 102. 8°. Dated A.D. 1882.

Or. 4089. A work on Syriac Grammar in verse form (the headings of the different parts being also given in Karshuni) entitled ܗܒܒ ܝ̈ܕܥܬܐ, or "The Flower of Sciences," by the Presbyter Jacob ܡܛܪܒܠܝܐ (of ܡܛܪܒܘܠ; see Sachau, Kurzes Verzeichniss . . . Syrischer Handschriften, no. 93. — Also see Or. 4438 in this List. — A metrical discourse on the Trinity and the Unity; alphabetical, two stanzas being assigned to each letter (beginning: ܐܝܬܝܐ ܕܚܝܠܝ ܒܡ ܗܘܝ̈ܐ).—Paper, foll. 74. Folio. xviiith Century.

Or. 4090. ܟܬܐܒ ܐܠܗܕܐܝܐ, the Nomocanon of Gregory Bar-Hebraeus (see Wright's "Syriac Literature," pp. 277-8), in Karshuni, to which is added a short account of fourteen Church Councils, also in Karshuni.—Paper, foll. 176 (in two columns). Folio. Dated A.GR. 2135=A.D. 1824.

Or. 4091. ܟܬܐܒ ܐܠܚܡܐܡܗ, or "Book of the Dove," a manual for Ascetics, by Gregory Bar-Hebraeus (for other MSS. of this work in Syriac and Arabic, see Wright's "Syriac Literature," p. 277, note 1), in Karshuni. Paper, foll. 73. Sm. 8°. xviiith Century.

Or. 4092. A Karshuni work on Christian Ethics, ascribed to Simeon the Stylite, *junior* (?), of Antioch. Another copy is Or. 2322, where also see references. Paper, foll. 205. Sm. 4°. Dated A.D. 1803.

Or. 4093. ܒܘܩ ܐܠܬܘܒܐ, a treatise on Repentance, in three parts, translated into Arabic (having Karshuni form in the present MS.) from a European language, under the superintendence of a French Franciscan monk of the name of Joseph, in the year 1717 A.D. (See Or. 5079, which contains the same work in the Arabic character.) Paper, foll. 226. Sm. 4°. xviiith Century.

Or. 4094. ܟܬܐܒ ܣܒܒ. ܟܠ ܐܠܐܣܒܐܒ., a Karshuni translation of the well-known Syriac work ܥܠܬ ܟܠ ܥܠ̈ܠܐ (i.e. Causa Causarum), attributed in the present MS. (fol. 201*a*) to Jacob of Edessa (see, however, Kayser's German translation, "Das Buch der Erkenntniss der Wahrheit," &c., pp. xix., xx.). The translator's name, 'Abd al-Nūr al-Amidī, is given on fol. 2*b*; but the translation of only seven Maḳālāt is here given. Paper, foll. 202. Folio. Dated A.GR. 2163 = A.D. 1852 = A.H. 1268.

Or. 4095. A manual of Medicine, partly derived from Persian, Turkish, Greek, and French sources, by the

Deacon Thomas. Karshuni. Paper, foll. 185. Sm. 4°. xixth Century.

Or. 4096. ܐܣܡܐ ܐܠܐܕܘܝܗ ܐܠܡܦܪܕܗ̈, a Dictionary of "Simple Medicaments" (a recension (colophon, fol. 329*a*) of a portion of Dā'ūd al-Anṭākī's Tadkirah), in Karshuni. Paper, foll. 330. Sm. 4°. xviiith Century.

Or. 4097. A Syriac and Arabic Lexicon (the Arabic taking the Karshuni form), compiled from the Lexicon of Bar-Bahlūl by the Maphrian Simeon al-Ṭūrānī. It is stated in the colophon (fol. 137*b*) that the compiler omitted the Greek words and only retained the Syriac ones; but this principle has not been consistently followed in the work itself. Paper, foll. 137. Sm. folio. Dated A.D. 1886.

Or. 4098. The Syriac and Arabic Lexicon of Ḥasan bar Bahlūl. Paper, foll. 394. Folio. Dated A.D. 1883.

Or. 4395. The Books of Isaiah, the Minor Prophets, Jeremiah, Ezekiel, Daniel, and Bel and the Dragon. Peshiṭta version, with Nestorian pointing. Some ornamentations. Paper, foll. 224. Folio. Dated A.GR. 2124 = A.D. 1813.

Or. 4396. The Books of Joshua, Judges, Samuel, Kings, Proverbs, Ecclesiastes, Ruth, Song of Songs, Ben Sira, and Job. Peshiṭta version, with Nestorian pointing. Some ornamentations. Paper, foll. 269. Folio. Dated A.GR. 2119 = A.D. 1808.

Or. 4397. The first, second, and third Books of the Maccabees, Chronicles, Ezra-Nehemiah, Wisdom, Judith, Esther, Susannah, and the Epistles of Jeremiah and Baruch (Peshiṭta, with Nestorian pointing), followed by Tobit in a Syriac version made in 1818 from an Arabic version of the Vulgate, by a priest of the name of Petros Asmar, of Tell-Kēfē. Paper, foll. 267. Folio. Dated A.D. 1852.

Or. 4398. ܟܬܒܐ ܕܣܘܢܗܕܘܣ ܬܒܝܠܝܬܐ ܕܩܢܘܢܐ ܫܠܝܚܝܐ ܘܩܕܝܫܐ, followed (fol. 21*b* sqq.) by ʽEbed-Yēshūʽ bar Bĕrīkhā's "Selection of Synodical Canons" (see Assem., Bibl. Orientalis, iii., pp. 332—351, and Mai, Scriptt. Vett. Nova Coll., x.). At the end (fol. 142*a* sqq.) are the following small pieces: 1. ܥܠܠ ܫܘܐܠܐ (questions relating to canonical rules). 2. ܥܠܠ ܘܗܘܪܐ ܕܡܫܒܚܢܐ 3. ܡܡܠܠܐ ܕܐܦܝܠܘܦܘܣ (beg. ܟܠ ܗܠܝܢ ܦܠܓ ܡܪܬ ܠܟ). 4. ܥܠܠ ܡܩܪܐ ܕܡܒܝܢܝܢ ܠܐܟܘܢ ܘܩܢܝܐ ܡܪܝ ܕܐܝܣܝܕܘܪܘܣ ܕܡܝܢ ܒܪ ܟܠܝܒ.—Paper, foll. 152. 4°. Dated A.D. 1890.

Or. 4399. A Choral Service-book, described in the heading (fol. 1*b*) as: ܟܬܐ ܡܦܩܕܢܐ ܕܟܠܗ ܫܢܬܐ . ܐܝܟ ܦܢܩܝܬܐ ܕܐܚܝܕ ܘܪܕܐ ܘܡܬܡܫܠ ܒܡܩܦܠ ܡܛܝܒܘܬܐ ܢܒܐܬܐ . ܕܡܬܚܕܕ ܦܢܩܝܬܐ ܕܕܪܐ ܒܠܝܬܐ ܕܡܪܝ ܟܢܘܫܬ ܘܡܪܝ ܐܒܪܗܡ: First heading: ܡܫܡܫܬ . ܕܐܦܝܐ ܕܠܝܠܐ. Imperfect at the end. Paper, foll. 578. Dated (fol. 377*a*) A.GR. 1800 (A.D. 1489).

Or. 4400. An ancient copy of the Pentateuch according to the Peshiṭta, apparently of the viith or viiith Century, but restored A.D. 1684. The lectionary marks are also by a later hand. Vellum (but the later portions are on paper), foll. 178. Folio.

Or. 4401. A Glossary of a Modern Syriac dialect (Fellihī). The copyist signs his name on fol. 258*a* as

ܐܝܫܥܝ, ܕܡܠܟ ܝܘܢܢ ܕܓܘܓܬܦܗ, Eshai Malik Yonan Geog Tapa, Oroomiah, Persia. Paper, foll. 258. 4°. Dated A.D. 1890.

Or. 4402. The Chronicle of Michael, the elder, in Karshuni. Syriac title (fol. 1*b*): ܟܬܒܐ ܕܡܟܬܒܢܘܬ ܙܒܢܐ ܕܣܝܡ ܘܡܦܠܣܗ ܠܡܪܝ ܡܝܟܐܝܠ ܪܒܐ ܦܛܪܝܪܟܐ ܕܣܘܪ̈ܝܝܐ ܕܒܥܕܢܗ ܘܡܦܩܗ ܡܢ ܟܬܒܐ ܕܡܪܝܒܪܘܣ ܟܠܕܝܐ ܘܡܘܣܪܦܝܢܘܣ ܘܐܬܘܕܘܪܘܣ ܘܓܒܪ. In the colophon on fol. 420*a* it is stated that the Arabic translator (from the Syriac) of this ܡܟܬܒ. ܙܒܢܐ or ܬܐܘܪܝܟ ܐܠܙܡܐܢ was the ܡܦܪܝܐܢ named ܫܗܝܐ ܐܠܓܕܕ̈ܝ ܐܒܢ ܚܢܝܢ ܡܦ̄ܪܝܢ ܕܡܥܠܡ ܐܠܡܥܠܡ. On the Armenian version and the French translation that was made from it, see Wright's "Syriac Literature," p. 252. On a MS. of the original Syriac, see Guidi, Giornale della Soc. Asiat. Italiana, vol. iii., pp. 167—9. An edition of the Syriac is now being prepared by M. Chabot (Paris). Paper, foll. 422. Folio. Dated A.D. 1846.

Or. 4403. I. Discourses and stories of Saints, in Karshuni (imperfect at the beginning): (*a*) a homily of St. Chrysostom ܥܠܝ ܬܐܘܒܠ ܐܠܐܫܪܐܪ ܐܠܐܠܗܝܗ (fol. 7*a*); (*b*) a homily of Jacob of Serūg ܥܠܝ ܢܘܚ ܐܠܡܪܐܒܝܢ ܠܠܐܡܘܐܬ (fol. 15*b*); (*c*) a tract, by Dionysius bar Ṣalībī, entitled ܦܘܫܩܐ ܕܬܐܘܪܝܐ ܕܩܘܪܒܐ ܘܓܒܪ (fol. 30*a*; another copy is contained in Or. 2307; see Wright's "Syriac Literature," p. 248); (*d*) a eulogy ܥܠ ܐܒܘܢܐ ܡܪܝܣ (fol. 95*b*); (*e*) ܡܐܡܪ ܐܠܩܕܝܣܗ ܐܦܪܝܡܘܢܐ ܥܢ ܐܠܡܠܟ ܥܒܕ ܐܠܠܗ ܘܡܐ ܓܪܐ ܠܗܐ (fol. 105*a*; beg. ܩܐܠ ܐܢ ܦܝ ܕܐܠܟ ܐܠܙܡܐܢ ܓܠܝܠ ܡܠܟ); (*f*) ܡܐܡܪ ܐܠܡܠܟ ܝܘܢܢ

ܘܩܨܬܗ ܙܝܢܘܢ ܐܠܡܠܟ[a] (fol. 112*b*).—II. The Canons of Dionysius bar Ṣalībī (fol. 147*a*; compare Or. 4398, fol. 147*b* sqq).—Paper, foll. 185. 8°. Part I. belongs to the xiiith—xivth Century, and Part II. to the xviith Century.

Or. 4404. A collection of Lives of Saints, Martyrdoms, and stories of the Holy Cross, in the following order: The martyrdoms of Mār Cyriacus and his mother Julita (fol. 1*b*); the martyrdoms of Mār George, Antoninus ܐܣܛܪ̈ܛܠܛܝܣ (στρατηλάτης), and the Empress Alexandra (fol. 16*a*); the story of the father of Mār George (fol. 24*b*); the martyrdom of Behnam, son of Sennacherib, and of Sarah his sister (fol. 26*a*); the story of Mār Micah, of Nuhadra (ܕܐܬܝܠܕ ܗܘܐ ܒܡܕܝܢܬܐ ܒܟܘܠܣܐ ܒܪܐ ܕܚܕ ܡܢ ܢܝ̈ܢܘܐ ܕܒܓܘܪܒܝܐ, fol. 46*b*); the story of Abraham Ḳīdūnāyā (here, ܦܝܕܘܢܝܐ, fol. 57*b*); the story of Mār Ephrem (ܫܝܪܬܐ ܘܡܠܦܢܘܬܐ ܕܡܦܫܩܢܝܬܐ ܕܒܐܘܪܗܝ ܕܒܝܬ ܢܗܪܝܢ, fol. 73*a*); the story of the Apostles Matthew and Andrew (fol. 79*b*); the story of the eight (instead of the usual seven) sleeping children of Ephesus (fol. 87*b*); the story of Daniel ܐܣܝܐ (beg. ܣܒܝܒ ܘܗܡ ܠܡ ܕܝܬܘܒܠ ܒܡܕܝܢܬܐ ܕܒܝܫܝܡ, fol. 98*b*); the story of John ܒܪ ܡܠܟܐ (beg. ܒܥܝܢܐ ܪܒܐ ܕܦܘܪܢܣܐ ܕܡܠܟܐ, fol. 111*b*); the martyrdom of Mār Ya'ḳub ܡܦܣܩܐ, i.e. intercisus (fol. 121*a*); the story of the first finding of the Holy Cross by Protonicē, wife of the Emperor Claudius (fol. 128*b*); the story of the second finding of the Holy Cross by the Empress Helena after the Jews had taken it away from Simeon,

[a] I.e., the story of Hilaria, daughter of the Emperor Zeno and his wife Shams al-Munīr.

Bishop of Jerusalem, and hidden it (fol. 131*b*); the story of Mār Ḳardāg the martyr (fol. 141*b*); the story of the Cross of Christ, mocked by the Jews in the city of Tiberias in the days of the Emperor Zenon (fol. 166*b*). Paper, foll. 199. Folio. xixth Century.

Or. 4405. A Choral Service-book, beginning with a hymn on the Annunciation, and ending with a Karshuni hymn that is to be said ܩܕܐܡ ܐܠܩܪܒܐܢ. The greater part of the MS. was written A.GR. 1999 (A.D. 1688), and the rest (fol. 69 sqq.) was written shortly after by the same hand. Some missing leaves at the beginning have been supplied by a recent copyist. Paper, foll. 87. 8°.

Or. 4406. The Syriac and Arabic Lexicon of Bar-Bahlūl. Paper, foll. 340. Folio. Dated A.GR. 2196 (A.D. 1885).

Or. 4407. ܟܬܒܐ ܕܐܝܬܝܩܘܢ of Gregory Bar-Hebraeus. —A metrical composition by John b. Andrew (beg. ܠܟ ܠܒܢܐ ܡܦܪܝܫܐ ܡܫܝܚ ܗܘܝܬ; for other writings of this author see Wright's Cat., pp. 394, 395, &c.), followed by a series of metrical pieces, by Isaac of Antioch, and a poem by Jacob of Serūg on Ezekiel's vision.—Paper, foll. 194 (two columns to a page). Dated (fol. 157*b*) A.GR. 1887 (A.D. 1576); but a number of pages are quite recent.

Or. 4408. A book of Prayers in Karshuni, including ܡܥܐܬܐܝܬܗ ܘܐܟܠܝܠ ܦܝ ܐܠܩܕܐܣܐܬ ܘܐܠܬܩܪܒܐܬ (fol. 12*b*); ܡܕܝܚܗ ܡܪܬܒܗ ܠܠܥܕܪܐ ܐܠܡܛܘܒܗ (alphabetical, fol. 18*a*); ܬܣܒܚܗ ܬܩܐܠ ܩܕܐܡ ܐܠܩܪܒܐܢ ܦܝ ܝܘܡ ܐܠܐܚܕ (fol. 22*b*, this hymn being followed by others of the same designation, for different occasions); ܬܪܬܝܒ ܩܘܠ ܦܝ ܚܒܫ ܐܠܐܦܪܢܓܝ ܐܠܐ ܒܪܝܘܬܗ (fol. 24*b*); readings at the occasion of a wedding and the burial of divers persons (fol. 26*b* sqq.); ܫܒܝܗ ܠܬܪܝ ܩܘܫܐ ܐܠܡܬܢܚܐ ܕܡܒܢܝܐ ܠܬܪܝ ܫܡܥܘܢ ܡܦܪܝܢܘܠܐ ܕܐܡܪ (fol. 42*b*, this piece being followed by various other metrical compositions to be used on different occasions); ܬܪܬܝܒ ܩܘܠ ܦܝ ܐܠܡܥܝܕܐܬ (fol. 65*a*, also followed by a number of similar pieces); ܒܪܐܢܗ ܩܘܠ ܥܠܝ ܐܠܡܝܬܐܒ ܘܐܠܡܠܝܚܝܢ (fol. 77*b*, followed by other pieces under the term ܒܪܐܢܗ); canons to be used at the Communion Service (fol. 93*b*); ܫܘܪܐܚܐܬ (fol. 105*b*).—Paper, foll. 110. 12°. xvith—xviith Century.

Or. 4409. ܟܬܒܐ ܕܐܝܬܝܩܘܢ of Gregory Bar-Hebraeus, in Karshuni; same translation as Or. 2318, where see references. Paper, foll. 171. Folio. xviith Century.

Or. 4410. ܟܬܐܒ ܡܢܐܪܗ̈ ܐܠܐܩܕܐܣ. of Gregory Bar-Hebraeus, in Karshuni. For the name of the translator (also contained in the present MS.), &c., see Cat. Cod. Or. Bibl. Bodl., tom. ii., p. 451 sqq. See also Or. 4428. At the end is a list of twelve works, with the heading: ܫܡ̈ܗܐ ܕܟܬܒ̈ܐ ܕܣܡ ܣܘܪܝܬܐ ܘܡܠܝܠܘܬܐ ܗܘ ܡܪܢܝܐ ܐܒܘܢ ܡܪܝ ܓܪܝܓܘܪܝܘܣ.—There are illuminations at the beginning and end of the volume. Paper, foll. 213 (two columns to a page). Folio. Dated A.GR. 2007 (A.D. 1696).

Or. 4411. ܟܬܒܐ ܕܙܠܝܩܐ, or "Book of Rays," a compendium of theology, by Gregory Bar-Hebraeus. Paper, foll. 195. 8°. A.D. 1889.

Or. 4412. ܟܬܒܐ ܕܣܘܕ ܣܘܦܝܐ of Gregory Bar-Hebraeus.—A rhymed allegorical poem in 80 stanzas, by the same author, entitled ܡܐܡܪܐ ܕܥܠ ܚܟܡܬܐ ܐܠܗܝܬܐ (Carmen de Divina Sapientia; on the MSS. and editions, see Wright's "Syriac Literature," p. 280). The ܦܘܫܩ ܪ̈ܡܙܐ ܘܡ̈ܠܐ of the piece is given in the margin.—Paper, foll. 43. 8°. A.D. 1889-90.

Or. 4413. ܟܬܒܐ ܕܣܘܕ ܣܘܦܝܐ of Gregory Bar-Hebraeus, in Syriac and Arabic.—ܟܬܒܐ ܕܒܒ̈ܬܐ "Book of the Pupils of the Eyes," a compendium of the art of logic or dialectics, by the same author.—ܡܐܡܪܐ ܕܥܠ ܗܝܡܢܘܬܐ, a metrical discourse on faith, by Isaac of Antioch.—Paper, foll. 69. 8°. xixth Century.

Or. 4414. The book of Hierotheos: contents selected, arranged, and commented upon by Gregory Bar-Hebraeus. The preface is not given, and the work is incomplete at the end. Compare Or. 1017, fol. 120*b* sqq.; and see Wright's "Syriac Literature," pp. 76, 206, 277; also Forthingham, Stephen Bar Sudaili, p. 87, sqq. Paper, foll. 90. 8°. xixth Century.

Or. 4415. ܟܬܒܐ ܕܡܪܓܢܝܬܐ, or "Book of the Pearl," a theological work in five sections, by 'Ebed-Yēshū' Bar Bĕrīkhā. For references to Assemani's analysis of its contents, the edition of the text, and the Latin and English translations, see Wright's "Syriac Literature," p. 286. Paper, foll. 81. 12°. xvth—xvith Century.

Or. 4416. A Book of Funeral Services (ܕܥܢ̈ܝܢܐ ܐܘ ܒܝܬ ܕܩܘܒ̈ܪܐ), comprising (1) ܠܥܢܝܕܐ ܕܥܠ ܓܒܪ̈ܐ (fol. 1*a*;

imperfect at the beginning); (2) ܠܟܘܫܐ ܕܬܪܝܢ ܕܐܬܬܘܡܘܗܝ ܕܒܥܘܬܐ ܕܢܝ̈ܢܘܝܐ (fol. 72*a*); (3) ܠܟܘܫܐ ܕܬܠܬܐ ܕܟܠ ܠܠܝܐ ܒܫܒ̈ܝܢܐ (fol. 87*b*); (4) ܠܟܘܫܐ ܕܒܥܘܬܐ ܕܠܠ̈ܝܐ ܕܠܐ ܡܚܠܘ ܪܘܫܡܐ ܕܡܫܒܚܐ (fol. 124*a*); (5) a number of other Offices or portions of Offices, including ܠܟܘܫܐ ܕܐܡܬܝ ܕܡܫܬܥܐ ܡܫܬܥܝܬܐ ܡܢ ܡܕܪܐ ܠܡܕܪܐ, and various compositions, among which are ܡܕܪ̈ܫܐ composed by Yēshū'-yabh, Metropolitan of Arbel (fol. 140*b* sqq.), and by Israel, a priest of Alkōsh. — Paper, foll. 173. 8°. Dated Teshrin, A.GR. 2032 (A.D. 1720).

Or. 4417. The Pentateuch in the Peshitta version, with Nestorian pointing. Paper, foll. 233. Folio. Dated A.D. 1804.

Or. 4418. ܟܬܒܐ ܕܡܬܢ̈ܝܬܐ ܕܣܝܡ ܘܡܟܢܫ ܠܐܠܝܐ ܕܢܝܪܐ ܘܡܬܪ̈ܓܡܢܐ ܟܠܕܝܐ ܕܡܪܝ ܗܘܪܡܝܙܕ ܦܪܘܫܐ, a book of 30 poetical compositions in the form of short Maḳāmāt, by Elias, a Chaldaean (Romanist) monk of the convent of Mār Hormizd. The colophon on fol. 92*a* informs us that the author himself wrote out a copy of his work in the month Nīsān of the year 1886, and from fol. 92*b* it appears that the present copy was made later on in the same year. Explanatory notes accompany the compositions. — Bar-Hebraeus on ܒܝܬ ܡܠܐ ܕܫܘ̈ܝܬܐ (De vocibus aequivocis), forming Section V. of his metrical grammar (see Or. 4088). The present MS. is without the scholia. Paper, foll. 114. 8°. Also in a recent hand.

Or. 4419. Dissertations, in metrical form, mainly on religious subjects,[a] by Elias, Bishop of Pērōz Shābhōr

[a] See also Or. 4077.

or al-Anbar. The contents agree with the description found in Assemani, B. O., iii., pp. 258—60 of the ܬܠܬ ܦܘܢ̈ܝܬܐ ܒܡܘܫ̈ܚܬܐ mentioned by ʻEbed-Yēshūʻ. See also Wright's "Syriac Literature," p. 230. Paper, foll. 199. Folio. A.D. 1882.

Or. 4420. ܛܟܣܐ ܕܥܢܝ̈ܢܐ ܕܒܢܝ̈ ܥܠܡܐ ܕܓܒܪ̈ܐ ܘܕܢܫ̈ܐ ܘܕܛܠܝ̈ܐ ܐܝܟ ܛܟܣܐ ܕܕܝܪܐ ܥܠܝܬܐ ܕܡܪܝ, a book of Funeral Services, similar to the one described under Or. 4416. Paper, foll. 136. 8°. xviiith Century; but foll. 1—33 and some other leaves are quite recent.

Or. 4421. Another copy of the Services contained in the preceding number. Paper, foll. 119. xviiith Century; but some of the leaves are quite recent.

Or. 4422. A book of Sacred Poems[a] (entitled ܟܬܒܐ ܕܕܘܪ̈ܟܝܬܐ), in modern Syriac, the authors named in connection with different compositions being ܩܫܫ ܩܫܝܡ ܐܦܣܩܘܦܐ ܬܠܟܐܦܢܝܐ, ܒܪ ܡܩܕܣܝܐ ܓ̰ܠܝܡ ܕܗܘܪ̈ܐ, and ܩܫܡ ܬܘܡܣܝܢܐ. A piece beginning on fol. 100*b* is headed: ܕܘܪܟ ܕܐܪܡܝܢܘ ܡܠܟܐ ܓ̰ܡܓ̰ܡܐ (Jumjumah), and on fol. 103*b* begins a poem headed: ܕܘܪܟ ܕܡܫܝܚܐ ܘܕܟܢܫ̈ܗ. The writers

[a] On the kind of literature that is contained in this and the following number, and also on most of the authors here named, see Sachau, Über die Poesie in der Volkssprache der Nestorianer (Sitzungsberichte der Kön. Pr. Akad. der Wissenschaften zu Berlin, 1896, xi.); also Skizze des Fellichi-Dialects von Mosul, by the same author (Berlin, 1895); Mark Lidsbarski, Die neu-Aramaischen Handschriften der Kön. Bibliothek zu Berlin (Semitistische Studien, Heft 4/9). Compare also Guidi, Beiträge zur Kenntniss des neu-aramäischen Fellīḥi-Dialektes (Z.D.M.G., xxxvii., p. 293 sqq).

of the poems in this and the following number were members of the Roman Communion.—Paper, foll. 115. 8°. A.D. 1989 (for 1889).

Or. 4423. A book of Sacred Poems, similar to those described under the preceding number, the authors of compositions being the Priest ܗܘܪܡܝܙܕ ܬܘܡܢܝܐ, ܬܐܘܡܐ ܫܢܓܪܝ[a] ܬܠܟܝܦܢܝܐ, the Priest ܕܡܝܢܘܣ ܐܠܩܘܫܢܝܐ (writing in the year 1856), and the Priest ܝܘܣܦ.—Paper, foll. 143. 8°. About the same date as the preceding number.

Or. 4424. ܡܐܡܪܐ ܕܝܘܢܝܐ of Gregory Bar-Hebraeus, with additions by Khamīs bar Ḳardāḥe; Yēshū'-yahb, Metropolitan of Arbel (A.GR. ܐܫ̈ܣܓ = A.D. 1452); Yūsuf II., Patriarch of the Chaldaeans of Tell-Kēfē (A.GR. ܐܪ̈ܛ = A.D. 1698); and the Priest ܝܘܣܦ of ܬܠܟܦ.—ܡܐܡܪܐ ܕܥܠ ܡܠܟܘ ܐܣܟܝܡܘܬܐ ܘܠܒܘܫܗ ܬܘܒܐ ܕܟܗܢ ܦܘܪܫܢܐ, by Yūsuf II., Patriarch of the Chaldaeans, composed in the year 1698 A.D. = 2009 A.GR. —Paper, foll. 99. 8°. A.D. 1886.

Or. 4425. ܬܦܣܝܪ ܐܠܣܦܪ ܠܠܐܘܝܝܢ ܘܬܦܣܝܪܗ ܡܢ ܦܨܠ ܡܪܝ ܩܝܪܠܠܘܣ[b], the Book of Leviticus, in an Arabic (Karshuni) translation with Commentary, by an author of the name of Cyril (possibly Cyril, the 67th Patriarch of Alexandria, A.D. 1078—1092; or Cyril, the 75th Patriarch of the same see, A.D. 1235—1243. See Renaudot, Hist. Patr. Alex., pp. 449 and 576 sqq.).

[a] The same as Thomas Singārī in Sachau and Lidsbarki.

[b] The first ܩ appears, however, to have been corrected into ܟ.

The work is at any rate of post-Muhammadan date. Paper, foll. 139. 8°. A.GR. 2137 (A.D. 1826).

Or. 4426. ܒܪܗܐܢ̈ܗ ܐܣܪܐܪ ܐܠܐܠܗܝ̈ܗ, a Karshuni work in eight Makālāt, by the Maphrian Basil, also called Shem'on aṭ-Ṭūrānī (see the next number; also Or. 2325). Paper, foll. 127. 8°. A.GR. 2040 (A.D. 1729).

Or. 4427. ܣܠܐܚ ܐܠܥܠܡ ܘܬܪܣ ܐܠܥܘܡ, a Karshuni treatise (in 16 chapters) in defence of the doctrines of the Jacobites against the Nestorians and Romanists, by the author of the preceding work; composed A.D. 1724 (see no. 58 in Sachau, Kurzer Verzeichniss der Sachau'schen Sammlung syrischer Handschriften, Berlin, 1885). Paper, foll. 123. Folio. A.D. 1890.

Or. 4428. ܟܬܐܒ ܡܟܬܨܪ̈ܗ ܐܠܐܕܘܐܠ, by Gregory Bar-Hebraeus, in Karshuni. See Or. 4410.—Foll. 365—372 contain a number of stories in Syriac, beginning with ܬܫܥܝܬܐ ܕܬܘܡ ܐܢ̈ܫܐ ܘܚܠ ܙܪ̈ܘܢܐ ܦܘ̈ܪܫܢܐ, and ending with ܒܬܘܒܬܐ ܐܘܣܦܬ ܬܫܥܝܬܐ ܕܩܠܘܕܝܘܣ ܢܟܠܟܐ. Paper, foll. 372. 4°. A.D. 1887.

Or. 4429. Portions of (ܡܠܠ ܡܢ) the ܟܬܐܒ ܐܠܐܟܬܝܐܪ (comp. Mai, Script. Vet. Nova Collectio, tom. 4, nos. 74 and 117), compiled by Petros al-Jamīl, Bishop of Melij, also known by the name of Severus al-Jamīl. The different portions are: (1) on ܟܬܒ ܐܡܘܬܢܐ ܐܠܐܡܪ ܡܢ ܬܘܕܡܬܗܡ ܐܠܡܥܘܕܝܐ ܐܠܦܠܣܦܝ ܘܓܝܪܗܡ ܐܝܣܐ ܡܢ ܡܫܪܝ ܬܥܠܝܡܗܡ, by Petros al-Jamīl (ܐܢܒܐ ܦܛܪܣ); (2) Confession of faith (ܐܡܢܘܢ̈ܗ) of Severus of Antioch; (3) ܕܟܪ ܐܠܡܓܠܣܐ ܘܡܢ ܟܐܢ ܘܡܐ ܐܠܡܫܒܒ; (4) ܡܢ ܐܠܡܘܬܡܪܝܡ ܐܠܐܩܘܐܠ ܟܬܐܒ

ܘܫܪ̈ ܐܠܐܣܩܦܝܗ ܐܦܬܪܐܩ ܩܒܠ ܡܢ ܐܠܬܐܣܥܗ; (5)
ܘܫܪ̈ ܐܠܟܢܝܣܗ ܐܦܬܪܐܩ ܚܠ ܥܠܝ ܬܡܐ ܣܦܪ; (6)
ܦܝ ܘܢܝܗ̈ ܐܠܐܒ̈ ܐܠܡܣܝ̈ܚ ܐܒܢܐ ܘܐܠܪܘܚ ܐܠܩܕܣ
ܘܫܪ̈ ܐܠܡܓܐܠܣ ܟܬܐܒ ܐܝܣܐ ܐܠܟܬܒ ܗܕܐ; (7)
ܐܠܡܓܐܡܥ ܘܥܝܕ ܟܐܢ ܗܕܕ ܐܠܟܢܝܣܗ ܦܝ ܕܠܟ.
ܘܗܘ ܐܝܨܐ ܩܘܠ ܡܢ ܬܐܠܝܦ ܐܠܐܒ̈ ܐܠܩܣ̈ ܡܪܩܣ
ܐܠܐܦܣܘܣ ܐܣܩܦ ܐܠܐܦܣܘܣܝܢ ܡܢܥܘ ܟܐܢ
ܐܠܡܩܠ ܚܠܦ ܥܢܝ ܐܠܐܪܡܢܝܗ̈; (8) ܐܠܡܩܕܡܗ[a]
ܐܠܐܪܬܘܕܟܣܝܗ̈ ܐܠܬܝ ܟܬܒܗܐ ܟܡܐ ܐܠܣܘܐܪܝ
ܘܫܪ̈. The colophon at the end states that the MS. was copied A.D. 1890 from a codex that was written A.GR. 1766 (A.D. 1455). Paper, foll. 80.

Or. 4430. ܐܝܪܐܕ ܐܠܐܫܝܐ ܐܠܬܝ ܚܕܬܬ ܩܒܠ ܐܠܡܓܐܡܥ ܐܠܦܠܘܪܢܬܝܢܝ ܐܠܟܪܐܡ ܐܠܡܩܕܣܝܢ ܐܠܡܩܕܣܗ̈, an account, in Karshuni, of the events which took place before the sessions of the Florentine Council of A.D. 1441. Paper, foll. 267. A.D. 1818.

Or. 4431. ܟܬܐܒ ܐܠܡܓܐܠܣ, Karshuni disputations in seven sessions, held by Elias bar Shīnāyā with the vizir Abu'l-Ḳāsim al-Ḥusain in A.D. 1026, preceded by a short letter to the secretary Abu'l-'Ala Ṣā'id ibn Sahl. See Wright's "Syriac Literature," p. 238 (where also the reference to Assem. B. O. is given), and compare the Paris Catalogue of Arabic MSS., fasc. i., no. 82, 10.—The Nicene Creed with a Commentary (كتاب تفسير الامانة الكبيرة), the text of the Creed being in Syriac, and the Commentary in Arabic. Paper, foll. 147. Dated (fol. 121*b*) A.D. 1704.

[a] For ܒܐܣܡ ܐܠܡܩܕܡܗ.

Or. 4432. ܟܬܐܒ. ܐܠܡܘܐܠܝܕ ܘܐܠܡܘܠܘܕ ܡܢ ܬܐܠܝܦ ܐܒܘ ܡܥܫܪ ܐܠܡܫܗܘܪ. ܠܐܠܟܠܐܡ. ܐܠܦܠܟܝ ܘܐܠܡܢܓܡ, a work on the Horoscope, by Abū Ma'shar Ja'far ibn Muḥammad al-Balkhī. Paper, foll. 84. A.D. 1890.

Or. 4433. الارجوزة, a metrical compendium of medicine, composed in the metre Rajez, by Ibn Sina, with the Commentary of Ibn Rushd; Karshuni, the heading being in the Arabic character. Paper, foll. 128. 8°. A.GR. 2135 = A.D. 1825.

Or. 4434. Tracts on a fanciful classification of diseases according to the numerical value of names (ܚܘܫܒܢܐ ܕܚܠ ܟܪ̈ܝܗܐ), forecasts of various kinds, dreams and their interpretation, and some remedial preparations (ܡܠܟ ܣܦܪ ܡܣܡ̈ܢܐ ܐܣܝ̈ܘܬܐ). Paper, foll. 110. 8°. xixth Century.

Or. 4435. A book of Discourses for Festivals, by Yēshū' ibn Ibrāhīm ibn al-Yāmīn, of Malatia or Melitēne (ܐܝܫܘܥ ܐܒܢ ܐܒܪܐܗܝܡ ܐܒܢ ܐܠܝܐܡܝܢ ܡܢ ܡܠܐܛܝܐ), in the following order: (1) ܐܠܬܦܣܝܪ ܥܠܝ ܒܫܐܪ̈ܗ ܣܝܕܬܢܐ ܡܪܝܡ ܐܠܥܕܪܐ. (fol. 1b); (2) ܐܣܒܐܒ ܥܝܕ ܡܝܠܐܕ ܪܒܢܐ ܒܐܠܓܣܕ. (fol. 20b); (3) ܡܩܐܠܗ̈ ܕܓܛܐܣ ܡܫܝܚܐ ܐܠܡܥܠܡ (fol. 60b); (4) ܡܩܐܠܗ̈ ܝܘܡ ܡܫܝܚܐ ܐܠܐܪܒܥܝܢ (fol. 66b); (5) ܡܩܐܠܗ̈ ܓܒܪ ܥܝܕ ܥܢܨܪܗ ܐܠܐܣܪܐܪ ܘܫܪ (fol. 74b); (6) ܐܠܩܘܠ ܡܢ ܓܗܠ ܐܠܐܪܟܢ ܢܘܡ ܐܠܓܡܥܗ ܕܦܠܚܐ ܡܢ ܡܫ̈ܝܚܐ ܦܝ ܐܠܚܠܐܘܗ̈ ܒܥܕ ܡܢܐ ܐܟܠ ܐܠܟܐܪܘܦ ܐܠܢܐܡܘܣ. (fol. 84b); (7) ܡܩܐܠܗ̈ ܠܓܡܥܗ̈ ܐܠܐܠܐܡ (fol. 89a).—Paper, foll. 109. 8°. xixth Century.

Or. 4436. A collection of Karshuni tracts, imperfect at the beginning and the end. The extant headings are:

ܩܨ̈ܗ ܐܠܩܕܝܣܝܢ ܣܒܥܐ ܘܪܩܕܬܗ ܐܗܠ ܐܦܣܣ (i.e. the history of the seven sleepers of Ephesus; fol. 3*b*); ܓ̰ܕܕ ܡܢ ܟܬܐܒ ܐܠܐܫܐ ܐܠܐܣܬܐܕ ܐܠܕܝܢ ܦܝ ܟܠ ܝܘܡ (fol. 15*a*); ܩܨ̈ܗ ܕܐܢܝܐܝܠ ܘܐܠܦܬܝܗ (fol. 23*b*); ܩܨ̈ܗ ܐܠܩܕܝܣ ܡܪܝ ܩܘܪܝܐܩܘܣ ܘܘܐܠܕܬܗ ܝܘܠܝܛܐ, imperfect at the end (fol. 30*b*); on fol. 45*a* begins ܟܬܐܒ̈ ܐܠܟܢܘܙ (so in colophon on fol. 78*a*), not, however, agreeing with the ܡܥܪܬ ܓܙܐ (published by Bezold in 1888), but with the Book of Adam and Eve, I. and ch. i. of II. (published in English by S. C. Malan). The latter part (foll. 64*b* [end]—78*b*) forms part of another but similar work, in which Gregory Theologus is mentioned. On fol. 79*a* begins a fragment headed: ܚܒܪ ܡܢ ܩܘܠ ܡܪܐ ܐܦܪܝܡ ܐܠܡܠܦܢܐ ܘܗܘ ܥܠܝ ܡܚܒ ܡܠܟܝ ܐܠܐܚܒܐܒ ܘܐܠܐܚܒܐܒ. Paper, foll. 81. 8°. Dated A.GR. 2021=A.H. 1121 (A.D. 1710). The MS. is badly written.

Or. 4437. Religious tracts of the Monoptysite Church, including: ܡܪܬܫ̈ܗ ܥܠܝ ܐܠܐܡܪ ܡܥܕܘܢ ܘܡܚܠܝܠ ܘܦܪܝܫ ܘܡܠܐܟܐ ܘܡܘܬ ܐܠܡܣܝܚ (fol. 5*a*); ܬܦܣܝܪ ܐܠܐܡܐܢ̈ܗ ܐܠܐܒܘܐ ܐܠܐܪܬܘܕܘܟܣܝܝܢ ܥܢܝ ܐܠܐܡܐܢ̈ܗ ܘܬܒܐܢ̈ܗ (fol. 58*a*); questions and answers on theological terms (fol. 54*a*).—Appended is (fol. 109 sqq.) ܩܨ̈ܗ ܡܪܝ ܡܪܩܘܣ ܐܠܒܫܝܪ. Paper, foll. 170. Dated (fol. 108*b*) A.GR. 2157 (A.D. 1846).

Or. 4438. ܣܘܒܪܐ ܕܡܫܪ̈ܝܬܐ, a grammatical work, in verse form, by the Priest Jacob of ܩܛܪܒܠ, consisting mainly of various tables of inflections, in alphabetical order. The headings of the different parts are given both in Syriac and Karshuni. See also Or. 4089. Paper, foll. 70. Folio. xixth Century. Written by the author himself, who professes to imitate Jacob of Edessa and Gregory Bar-Hebraeus (ܥܠ ܕܘܡܝܐ ܐܘܪܗܝܐ ܘܡܥܢܝܢܐ ܡܠܦܢܐ).

Or. 4439. A book of Sacred Chants. Imperfect at the beginning and the end. The principal extant headings are: ܕܥܐܕܐ ܕܕܝܢܐ (fol. 10*a*); ܕܥܐܕܐ ܕܐܘܫܥܢܐ (fol. 23*b*); ܕܥܐܕܐ ܕܗܘܠܘܐ (fol. 59*b*); ܕܥܐܕܐ ܕܓܠܝܢܐ (fol. 75*b*). Paper, foll. 118. 12°. xixth Century.

Or. 4440. The Nestorian Marriage Service, the different portions being: ܛܘܥܝܬ ܒܪܘܬܐ, ܛܟܣܐ ܕܡܟܘܪܝܐ, ܛܟܣܐ ܕܒܘܪܟ ܓܢܘܢܐ, ܛܟܣܐ ܕܟܠܠܐ, ܘܛܟܣ ܓܘܢܝܐ. Paper, foll. 50. 12°. A.GR. 2158 (A.D. 1847).

Or. 4441. A volume of prayers (partly with lessons from the Holy Scriptures) for various occasions, in Karshuni; imperfect at the beginning. Among the headings are: ܨܠܐܗ ܥܠܝ ܐܠܡܝܬ ܘܠܠ ܕ.. ܢܦܣܗ (fol. 2*b*); ܨܠܐܗ ܥܠܝ ܐܠܡܝܬ ܠܠܟ ܥܦܐ ܐܠܐܡܪܐܬ (fol. 3*b*); ܨܠܐܗ ܐܠܬܘܒܐ ܥܠܝ ܟܠ ܐܢܣܐܢ ܦܪܝܐܢ ܘܡܩܪܘܒ (fol. 8*a*); ܨܠܐܗ ܥܠܝ ܐܠܐܥܬܪܐܦ ܐܠܟܒܝܪ (fol. 17*b*).—Fol. 76*a*—92*b* contain a series of seven prayers, the first three being by Basil the Great, and the last four by John Chrysostom. Paper, foll. 93. 12°. Dated A.GR. 2063 (A.D. 1752).

Or. 4442. The Psalter, in the Peshiṭta version, followed (fol. 117*a*) by Biblical canticles (ܬܫܒ̈ܚܬܐ ܕܡܘܫܐ ܘܕܐܫܥܝܐ), and (fol. 121*b*) ܬܫܒ̈ܚܬܐ ܕܚܘܕܪܐ:

embodying compositions by Ephrem Syrus; the Catholicos Timothy; Giorgis, Metropolitan of Nisibis; and others. The names of authors have, in several cases been erased (apparently from motives of Roman orthodoxy). Paper, foll. 170. xviiith Century (but foll. 1—14, 169—170 are quite recent).

Or. 4443. A Choral Service-book. Imperfect at the beginning and the end. The first extant heading (fol. 5*a*) is: ܡܥܢܝ̈ܬܐ ܕܟܠ ܕܡܪ̈ܢܝܬܐ ܕܥܒܕ ܡܪܢ ܘܐܠܗܢ ܝܫܘܥ ܡܫܝܚܐ. On fol. 52*b*: ܥܢܝ̈ܢ ܡܥܢܝ̈ܬܐ ܕܟܠܗܘܢ ܥ̈ܐܕܐ ܕܡܕܒܪܢܘܬܗ ܕܡܪܢ ... ܝܫܘܥ ܡܫܝܚܐ; from there to the end of the MS., a series of Services under the heading of ܠܚܘ̈ܣܐ ܕܒܝܬ ܐܠܗܐ. Paper, foll. 16. 12°. xvth Century.

Or. 4444. A small volume containing: (1) a ܬܫܒܘܚܬܐ by ܐܠܝܐ ܡܛܪܦܘܠܝܛܐ ܕܨܘܒܐ ܘܐܪܡܢܝܐ; (2) a metrical composition: ܥܠ ܡܥܡܘܕܝܬܐ ܕܢܚܬܐ by Ephrem Syrus; (3) ܦܘܪܫܢܐ ܗܘܐ ܕܡܢ ܣܘܢܗܕܘܣ ܕܢܝܩܘܣ ܕܥܠ ܚܢܢܐ ܟܗܢܐ ܕܒܢܝ ܠܡܫܝܚܐ ܐܘܣܒܝܘܣ ܐܦܣܩܘܦܐ ܕܦܠܣܛܝܢܐ; (4) ܡܠܠ ܡܘ̈ܫܐ ܕܡܫܡܫܝܢ ܠܥܠܝܡ̈ܐ ܘܐܬܗ̈ܡܬܐ ܠܛܘܒܐ. Paper, foll. 68. 12°. A.GR. 1983 (A.D. 1672).

Or. 4524. Expositions on most of the books of the Old Testament, by Yēshū'-dādh, Bishop of al-Ḥaditha, in the following order: Genesis, preceded by a general introduction (fol. 1*b*), Exodus (fol. 61*a*), Leviticus (fol. 79*a*), Numbers (fol. 87*a*), Deuteronomy (fol. 96*b*), Joshua (fol. 107*a*), Judges (fol. 112*a*), Samuel (fol. 119*b*), Kings (fol. 138*b*), Bar Sira (fol. 162*b*), Ecclesiastes (fol. 169*a*), Song of Songs (fol. 176*a*), Ruth (fol. 177*b*), Job (fol. 180*b*), Isaiah (fol. 190*a*), Minor Prophets (fol. 209*a*), Jeremiah (fol. 233*b*), Ezekiel (fol. 247*a*), Daniel (fol. 265*a*), Psalms (fol. 276*b*). The title of each exposition is ܦܘܫܩܐ. The author's name has in most cases been erased, but it has been preserved in the heading of Joshua and a few other instances. See Wright's "Syriac Literature," pp. 220-221.—Paper, foll. 330. Folio. xvii—xviiith Century.

Or. 4525. The Psalms, in the Peshiṭta version, provided with the arguments (ܥܠ̈ܠܬܐ) of Theodore of Mopsuestia, and the canons of Mār Abha the Catholicos; followed by the songs of Moses and Isaiah, and a collection of Church hymns for Sundays and festivals, &c., by Narsai, Ephrem Syrus, Babai the Great, and others. Paper, foll. 127. Folio. xixth Century.

Or. 4526. A volume containing: ܟܬܒܐ ܕܡܪܓܢܝܬܐ of 'Ebed-Yēshū' bar Bĕrikha (fol. 3*b*).—ܡܐܡܪܐ ܕܐܝܬ ܒܗ ܡܢܝܢܐ ܕܟܠܗܘܢ ܟܬܒ̈ܐ ܥܕ̈ܬܢܝܐ of the same author (fol. 37*a*). — ܟܬܒܐ ܕܠܘܩܛܐ ܕܡܬܩܪܐ ܕܕܒܘܪܝܬܐ of Solomon of Khilāṭ or Akhlāṭ, Metropolitan of Pĕrath dĕ-Maishān or al-Baṣrah (fol. 54*a*); see Mr. Budge's edition, and compare Or. 5281. — A series of smaller pieces, notably: ܬܫܒܘܚܬܐ ܬܫܥܝܬܐ ܕܓܒܪܐ ܦܠܘܬܒܢܐ (fol. 155*a*); ܬܫܒܘܚܬܐ ... ܕܦܝܠܠܘܣ ܥܠܝܡܐ ܘܡܣܟܢܐ (fol. 176*a*); ܬܫܒܘܚܬܐ ܕܐܢܫܐ ... ܫܕ ܕܦܪܒ ܗܘܐ ܬܫܒܘܚܬܐ (fol. 190*a*); ܬܫܒܘܚܬܐ ܕܐܡܪܐ ܐܢܫܝܡܘܣ ܘܕܐܒܠܐ ܕܐܬܓܠܝܘ ܠܦܪܘܣ̈ܝܐ ܕܐܠܟܣܢܕܪܝܐ (fol. 196*b*); ܐܓܪܬܐ ܕܢܕܫܒܥܐ ܘܢܕܥܐ ܕܢܫܬܬ ܡܢ ܥܒܪܝܐ ܥܠ ܐܝܕܝ ܡܪܝ ܐܬܢܣܝܘܣ (fol.

204a); ܬܫܥܝܬܐ ܕܡܪܬܝ ܡܪܝܡ ܠܒܝܬܘܬܐ (fol. 210a); the story of ܡܪܝ ܝܘܚܢܢ ܒܪ ܡܠܟܐ (fol. 258b); the martyrdom of ܡܪܝ ܩܘܪܝܩܘܣ ܘܐܡܗ ܝܘܠܝܛܐ (fol. 268a). — Paper, foll. 285. 8°. Dated A.GR. 2038 (A.D. 1727).

Or. 4527. Short religious compositions by monks of the convent of Rabban Biyyā, the whole being described in the colophon (foll. 99b, 100a) as: ܟܬܒܐ ܕܐܝܬ ܒܗ ܥܣܪ ܡܠܘܫܐ ܕܐܬܚܬܡܘ ܥܬܝܩܐ ܡܐܡܪ̈ܐ ܡܢ ܪ̈ܝܫܢܐ ܕܕܝܪܐ: ܡܢ ܡܐܡܪ̈ܢܐ ܕܟܠܗ: ܘܡܐܡܪ̈ܐ ܕܐܝܬ ܥܠܝܗ ܡܢ ܐܓܪ̈ܬܐ ܕܟܠ ܥܘܢܝ̈ܬܐ ܕܝܘܣܦ ܢܝ̈ܚܐ. Paper, foll. 100. 8°. A.GR. 2016 (A.D. 1705).

Or. 4528. A volume containing the history of Joseph, the son of Jacob, by Basil of Cesarea (see also Or. 2316); the history of Jacob, the Egyptian recluse (ܬܫܥܝܬܐ ܕܡܪܝ ܝܥܩܘܒ ܚܒܝܫܐ ܘܕܚܒܪ̈ܘܗܝ), fol. 26a); and a large number of short narratives, tracts in the form of questions and answers, &c. Paper, foll. 248. Sm. 8°. Dated (fol. 244a) A.GR. 2048 (A.D. 1737).

Or. 4599. Services for the dedication of a church (ܠܩܘܕܫܐ ܫܘܬܐܣܐ ܐܝܟ ܛܘܪܓܐ ܡܕܝܢܚܐ ܕܩܘܕܫܬܐ), the Annunciation of Zecharias, the Annunciation of the Blessed Virgin, &c. Written by several hands. Paper, foll. 194 (two columns to a page). Folio. xiiith-xivth Century. According to a note on the recto of the first leaf, the MS. changed hands A.GR. 1994 (A.D. 1683).

Or. 4600. ܠܚܘܕܪܐ ܕܡܫܡܫܢܐ ܕܡܫܡܫܢܘܬܐ ܡܢ ܒܥܕܐ ܕܕܢܚܐ ܒܥܕܢܐ ܠܦܘܩܕܢܐ ܡܪܐܢܝܐ, Commemoration of the repentance of Niniweh, Commemoration of the Dead, &c. Paper, foll. 346 (two columns to a page). Folio. Probably xvth Century. According to a Karshuni note on the recto of the first leaf, the MS. changed hands A.GR. 1877 (A.D. 1566).

Or. 4692. Fragment of a manual on Church doctrine, largely in the form of question and answer. Paper, foll. 51. 8°. xviith—xviiith Century.

Or. 4824. A portion of a Jacobite Lectionary from the Gospels, the greater part consisting of consecutive lessons from St. John in the Ḥarḳlensian version. Good writing of apparently the xith or xiith Century. Vellum, foll. 56. 12°.

Or. 4951. A volume containing the "Liturgy of the Nile" (see the printed edition, published by G. Margoliouth, Nutt, 1896), and Services to be used at the consecration of a church, the ordination of readers, subdeacons, &c. The prayers are for the most part in the Palestinian Syriac dialect, but several portions are in Greek in the Syriac character. The liturgical directions are in Karshuni. The ritual is that of the Malkite Church. Paper, foll. 70. Sm. 4°. Probably not later than the xiith Century.

Or. 5020. A copy of the Choral Service Book known as the "Octôêchus." Vellum, foll. 111. 8°. A.GR. 1491 (A.D. 1179).

Or. 5021. A fragment of the Life of St. Anthony.—The

Life of Paul of the Thebaid.—A letter of Anthimus. Vellum, foll. 34. 8°. A.GR. 1214 (A.D. 903).

Or. 5265. The Peshiṭta version of the New Testament, with Nestorian pointing. Vellum, foll. 288. 4°. A.GR. 1556 (A.D. 1245).

Or. 5281. A volume containing (1) a fragment of a work of magic prayers, etc.; (2) a large portion of the Book of the Bee (ends with ch. 47 of Mr. Budge's edition). See also Or. 4526. Paper, foll. 146. Sm. 4°. xviiith Century.

Or. 5441. ܡܡܠܠܐ ܕܥܠ ܐܠܗܘܬܐ ܘܥܠ ܐܢܫܘܬܐ, a work on the union of the two natures in our Lord, by Babai the Great, directed against the Monophysites (see Wright's "Syriac Literature," p. 168). Paper, foll. 206. Apparently of the xivth Century.

Or. 5442. A work on astrology, written in a peculiar hand. Paper, foll. 153. Sm. 4°. Probably xvith-xviith Century.

Or. 5443. The "Paradise of Eden," a collection of fifty poems on theological subjects, by 'Ebed-Yēshū' bar Bĕrikha, preceded by a list of the difficult words occurring in the work, together with explanations in modern Syriac. Paper, foll. 109. A.D. 1891.

Or. 5463. A volume containing 71 metrical discourses by Narsai. The metre is for the most part dodecasyllabic, but some of the discourses (e.g. no. 16, fol. 92*a*; 17, fol. 97*b*; 21, fol. 117*a*) are heptasyllabic (comp. Wright's "Syriac Literature," p. 58). After the 43rd discourse is the following colophon (fol. 219*b*) : ܫܘܠܡ ܡܐܡܪ̈ܐ ܕܡܬܒܪܢܘܬܐ ܕܡܬܐܡܪܝܢ ܒܣܘܕܪܐ ܕܟܠܗ ܫܢܬܐ : ܕܥܒܝܕܝܢ ܠܡܠܦܢܐ ܡܪܝ ܢܪܣܝ ܡܦܫܩܢܐ :. Then, at the head of the 44th homily: ܬܘܒ ܕܟܠܗ ܕܝ ܕܟܠܗ ܡܐܡܪ̈ܐ ܕܡܬܩܪܝܢ ܕܒܡܘܬܒܐ. At the end (fol. 352*b* sqq.): ܬܘܒ ܡܐܡܪ̈ܐ ܕܡܫܝܚܘܬܗ ܕܝܠܕܐ ܕܥܒܝܕ ܠܡܪܢ ܐܘܫܥܢܐ ܫܠܡ. ܒܘܝܢܐ ܡܠܘܫܐ ܒܒܢܝ ܕ̈ܝܪܐ. Paper, foll. 358. Large 4°. Dated Urmi, A.D. 1893.

INDEX OF NAMES.*

* Most of the Lives of persons are entered in this Index, but some will also be found under ܡܠܗ̈ and ܬܫܥܝܬܐ.

'Azīz bar Sābhĕtha (Patriarch Ignatius VII.). Or. 2308 (p. 7).
Babai the Great. Or. 4525 (p. 46).
———— Or. 5441 (p. 49).
Balaeus. *See* Balai.
Balai. Or. 4078 (p. 24).
Bar-'Alī. *See* Yēshū' bar 'Alī.
Bar-Bahlūl. *See* Ḥasan bar Bahlūl.
Barbara and Juliana; lives of. Or. 4436 (p. 43).
Bar-Hebraeus. *See* Gregory Bar-Hebraeus.
Basil, Bishop of Bagdad. *See* Philoxenus, Bishop of Bagdad.
Basil of Cesaraea. Or. 2316 (p. 9).
———— Or. 4065 (p. 20).
———— Or. 4441 (p. 44).
———— Or. 4528 (p. 47).
Basil, Maphrian. *See* Simeon al-Ṭūrānī.
Behnam, and his sister Sarah; martyrdom. Or. 4401 (p. 33).
Beh-Yēshū'. Or. 4527 (p. 47).
Bishō'. *See* Beh-Yēshū'.
Brīkh-Yēshū'. *See* Beh-Yēshū'.
Cyprianus, Mār. Or. 4066 (p. 21).
Cyriacus and Julita; martyrdom. Or. 4404 (p. 33).
————; martyrdom. Or. 4436 (p. 43).
————; martyrdom. Or. 4526 (p. 47).
Cyril of Alexandria. Or. 1272 (p. 2).
———— Or. 2319 (p. 10).
———— Or. 2321 (p. 11).
Mār Cyrillos; Karshuni commentary on Leviticus. Or. 4425 (p. 39).
Damianus of Alkōsh. Or. 4423 (p. 39).
Daniel, Medicus; life of. Or. 4404 (p. 33).
Daniel bar Ḥaṭṭāb. Or. 4087 (p. 27).
Dā'ūd al-Antākī. Or. 4096 (p. 30).
Denḥā, Catholicos of the Nestorians. Or. 4087 (p. 27).
Didacus de Estella. Or. 4073 (p. 23).
Dionysius the Areopagite. Or. 2306 (p. 6).
Dionysius bar Ṣalībī. Or. 2307 (p. 7).
———— Or. 4398 (p. 31).
———— Or. 4403 (pp. 32, 33).
Ebdochus (?). Or. 1594 (p. 3).
'Ebed-Yēshū' of Gāzartā. Or. 4071. (p. 22).
'Ebed-Yēshū' of Gāzartā Zabdaitā. Or. 4063 (p. 20).
'Ebed-Yēshū' bar Bĕrikha. Or. 2302 (p. 6).
———— Or. 2303 (p. 6).
———— Or. 4068 (p. 21).
———— Or. 4069 (p. 21).
———— Or. 4398 (p. 31).
———— Or. 4415 (p. 36).
———— Or. 4526 (p. 46).
———— Or. 5443 (p. 49).
Elias of al-Anbar. Or. 4077 (p. 24).
———— Or. 4419 (pp. 37, 38).

INDEX OF TITLES.

---

[a] See also Cambridge Add. MS. 2020, fol. 121*a* sqq.

CORRIGENDA.

On p. 5, under Or. 2297, omit "The first part of," at the beginning of the description.

On p. 47, under Or. 4599, instead of "Services for the dedication of a church," read "A Choral Service-book, containing:—"

On p. 60, col. 2, after ܟܬܒܐ ܕܚܘܕܪܐ, omit the words in [ ], and add "Or. 4599 (p. 47)."

www.ingramcontent.com/pod-product-compliance
Lightning Source LLC
Chambersburg PA
CBHW022151090426
42742CB00010B/1471
9783744735995